Greasy Grimy Gopher Guts:

The Subversive Folklore of Childhood

Greasy Grimy Gopher Guts:

The Subversive Folklore of Childhood

Josepha Sherman & T.K.F. Weisskopf

August House Publishers, Inc.
LITTLE ROCK

Printed in the United States of America

10 9 8 7 6 5 4 3 2 1   HB
10 9 8 7 6 5 4 3   PB

LIBRARY OF CONGRESS CATALOGING-IN-PUBLICATION DATA
Sherman, Josepha.
Greasy grimy gopher guts: the subversive folklore of childhood /
by Josepha Sherman and T.K.F. Weisskopf.
p.   cm.
Includes bibliographical references.
ISBN 0-87483-423-6 (hb : alk. paper). —ISBN 0-87483-444-9 (pbk. : alk. paper)
1. Children—United States—Folklore. 2. Folklore and children—United States.
3. Rhyming games—United States. I. Weisskopf, T.K.F. II. Title.
GR105.S48   1995
398'.083—dc20   95-34555

Executive editor: Liz Parkhurst
Project editor: Rufus Griscom
Design director: Ted Parkhurst
Cover design: Harvill Ross Studios Ltd.

AUGUST HOUSE, INC.   PUBLISHERS   LITTLE ROCK

AUTHOR WEISSKOPF:

To Gertrude Weisskopf,

who laughed when her grandchildren
provided her with a rendition of "How Dry I Am"

To Alexander M. Weisskopf,
who sang along enthusiastically

and

To my daughter, Katherine A.V. Baen,
who I hope will grow to appreciate these verses.

AUTHOR SHERMAN:

To the good folks of GEnie's SFRT
and WRITER'S .INK, without whom . . .

Acknowledgments

Such a book as this could not have been possible without the help of literally hundreds of informants who overcame whatever embarrassment they may have felt and shared their childhood with us. Thanks are due to all of you.

Special thanks go to the teachers and students of Park Hill Elementary School in North Little Rock, Arkansas for letting Author Sherman into their classrooms and to Hilary and the other librarians at Mamaroneck Public Library in Westchester, New York. Special thanks go to the managers of the following bookstores, where we also collected data: Tiku, Borders, Bohemia, Long Island; Mary, Barnes & Noble, West Paterson, New Jersey; and Irina, Barnes & Noble, Parmaus, New Jersey

Thanks are due to all the folks on GEnie, especially the sysops and the lurkers who came out from hiding in the Science Fiction Forum and provided so many of these rhymes. Thanks as well to those on America Online and the Internet, and to those in SFPA, whose rhymes were the first to be collected.

Thanks also to our editor, Liz Parkhurst, and the staff of August House, for letting this project see light of day.

Author Weisskopf would like to thank her mother, Vera Joan Hanfmann Weisskopf, for forever replacing the words to "Alma Mater" with those of "Weetamo, the Camp of Stinkers." She would also like to acknowledge the influence of Steven Brett, who was the source for so many rhymes at P.S. 241, and that of Professor Ronald Casson, professor of anthropology at Oberlin College.

Finally, we must thank our families and our coworkers at

Baen, not only for being treasure houses of great subversive verse, but also for putting up with us during this process even though they weren't obsessed by greasy grimy gopher guts too.

Contents

Introduction

The world can be a frightening, confusing place for children. Hemmed in by all its rules, whether natural laws or those laid down by adults, bombarded on all sides by entertainment and advertisements, scared and fascinated by such specters as Death, natural disasters, and crime, they strike back against the chaos in the only way they can: through folklore. Their songs and rhymes fearlessly take on the taboos and terrors of the adult world and turn them into things that can be safely mocked.

A similar pattern can be found in adult behavior around the world. The more rigid the society, the more the need for a chance to rebel—preferably in a way that the society can sanction. In the world of the Classical Greek, this escape took the form of the cult of Dionysus, which exalted drunkenness and freedom from rules. The European medieval societies enjoyed the wildness of the Lord of Misrule, a man who was chosen by lot each year, usually at the Winter Solstice or Christmas celebration, to rule over a brief period of complete reversal of the ordinary. Many other examples abound in the world's varied cultures.[1]

We see in both adult and children's folklore, for instance, the "sick joke." Whenever some natural or man-made disaster occurs that is simply too terrible to be confronted seriously, its sting is blunted by the sudden surge of these bizarre, stress-relieving forms of humor, whether the horror being parodied is the explosion of the Challenger shuttle or the AIDS epidemic.

In adult culture, however, such defiance of taboos is

always structured and limited; taboos are still in place. Children, on the other hand, have not only the sick joke, but also the offensive rhyme in their arsenal. While adults limit what can be discussed or mocked, no such sacred cows exist in the child's folkloric world. No subject is too fearful or disgusting; everything is interesting. And visiting this world is liberating both for the child who is hearing these songs for the first time and the adult who has them stored away in his or her memory.

This need to mock taboos goes a long way to explain the subversive elements of children's folklore. But why does it take the form of rhyme so often? Like the dirty joke, to be effective subversive verse must be shared—and a child's verse doesn't rely so much on delivery as an adult's joke to get its point across.[2] Which may also explain why most children remember these verses and can recite them years later: the use of rhyme makes verse easy to remember. But the utility of mnemonics doesn't fully explain the urge to make poetry, to use rhyme and meter and scansion. Versifying seems to be quite a deep instinct in humans. Even nonsense rhymes, such as verses rhyming Liberace with scotch (page 86) or Cheetah with amoeba (page 188), that play with sound as well as meaning, may be a key part of how children both learn and shape language. The verses collected below certainly show that rhyming is still a terrifically active force in children's folklore.[3]

Where do children learn their folkloric rhymes? Many of these rhymes have been learned at camp, with its combination of informality and campfire ritual an ideal place for the passing down of lore from older children (and sometimes even counselors) to younger ones. The schoolyard, too, in contrast to the more rigidly controlled classroom, is also a good place for children to transfer their private, "taboo" knowledge. An even better site than the schoolyard is the school bus. The bus is the ideal liminal location, not at school, not at home, not even at one place, but moving through space—the normal rules of school and home seem at least briefly to be suspended. On a more practical level, the bus is also a place where children can exchange their folklore safe in the knowledge that adults can't clearly overhear them, whether the topic of discussion is that most "dangerous" and fascinating of subjects, sex, or whether the goal is simply to gross each other out with an exchange of "greasy, grimy gopher guts."

When we first started putting this book together, we were both amazed at the response we received from those key words, "greasy, grimy gopher guts." Informants, whether adults or children, and no matter how reluctant to speak at first, came alive at this phrase and volunteered verse after verse. It was not unlike the phenomena of "memory cascade," usually associated with traumatic youthful incidents blocked out of memory. Once a single rhyme was recalled, almost invariably others would follow. Informants were also quite emphatic about making sure we had the "correct" version, although many would begin shyly, "I'm sure you have that one already."

While the phenomenon of subversive folklore is not by any means known only in the United States (one woman who had grown up in Madras was unfamiliar with "gopher guts," but when asked if children there had their subversive rhymes, said an emphatic, "Oh, yes!"—and gave a few examples in Tamil), we have limited our range to North America, with an emphasis on contemporary rhymes. All of the examples included in this volume have been collected first-hand between 1991 and 1994.[4] It is also important to remember that, shocking and graphic as many of these rhymes are, they were all collected from children or adults remembering verses they knew as children. Our youngest informants were five years old.

While we received samples from a wide variety of sources, we relied on two primary means of collection: 1) using computer networks, especially GEnie™, America Online™, and the Internet; and 2) going to schools, libraries, and children's bookstores across the country and talking directly to children. Since some informants were reluctant to have their full names included, we have used first names only. We feel we have a representa-

Introduction

tive sampling of verses, though of course hundreds more exist and are constantly being created. We would love to hear from our readers with more examples.

Whenever possible, we have traced the historical antecedents of the rhymes. It's particularly frustrating to play "track down the influences" when dealing with living, mutating folklore, but many of our examples can be dated to the creation of modern commercial or popular icons, and several to the very birth of this country and to roots in the Old World. Folklore is, after all, the lore of the folk, the one heritage we all, adults or children, have in common.

GETTING DOWN TO BASICS: FROM SNAKES TO WORMS

When we first enter the world, we know nothing of the boundaries of human culture and society, of life itself. But soon enough we learn the realities of birth and death. We also come face to face, sometimes directly, sometimes by innuendo or advertising, with that most fascinating, most fundamental, and often most taboo of human subjects: sex.

These most basic facts of life, procreation, and death are also the ones from which our adult American society tends to shy. And this reluctance to talk about such fundamental matters, ones that seem the most intriguing to children, can be one of the main sources of childhood frustration. Lacking concrete information about the way of coming into the world and faced with adult terror of leaving it, children cut through the Gordian Knot of the unknown and half-understood with the sword of folk rhymes. The mysteries of sex and birth are, if not truly demystified, at least made more familiar.

And even that most terrible of specters, Death, is cut down to size by such rhymes!

CHAPTER ONE:

GOPHER GUTS
AND OTHER GROSS-OUTS

One of the most common forms of children's folkloric rhymes is that known as the gross-out. While some gross-outs have an aim (those in Chapter Three, for instance, ridicule adult taboos about various bodily functions) many gross-out rhymes are intended almost entirely to shock. These general gross-outs often have little obvious "redeeming social value" and few specific subversive targets, but they still do serve a useful function. There are times when every child (and indeed every adult) thinks the world is allied against him or her. The gross-out rhymes exist as a means of letting off steam, rebelling against the societal strictures, food rules, and safety restrictions set by adults—and, in the process, thoroughly disgusting everyone listening. The gross-out is only effective if shared. These stories are told for the audience's reaction.[1]

The "Gopher Guts" Story

One of the most famous gross-out rhymes of all, at least in North America, is that which begins with some variation of the line "greasy, grimy gopher guts." No matter what their age, the informants were almost certain to volunteer at least a line or two. Although the ingredients listed in this rhyme vary from informant to informant, all the variants share the basic idea of eating utterly disgusting and incongruously combined substances. This is an all-purpose rhyme (which may help explain its popularity) that can be used as a general gross-out, a generic put-down of the opposite gender, a commentary on school food, or an insult against a specific target:

(to be sung to the tune of "The Old Grey Mare")

Version One:

Great green gobs of greasy, grimy gopher guts,
Mutilated monkey meat,
Little birdies' dirty feet.
Great green gobs of greasy, grimy gopher guts,
And I forgot my spoon.

♦ *Author Sherman, Bronx, New York, ca. 1960s. A version from Andy, Brooklyn, New York, ca. 1960s, shows the folk process in action: His otherwise almost identical version adds the line: "One quart can of all-purpose porpoise pus"—which has the added attraction of being a tongue twister as well as being revolting— before "And I forgot my spoon."*

Version Two:

Great big gobs of ooey, gooey gopher guts,
Oldy moldy goober nuts,
Little turdy birdie feet,
All wrapped up in marinated monkey meat,
And I forgot my spoon.
I forgot, oh I forgot my spoon.
(Repeat last line.)

♦ *Katherine, Connecticut, age ten, 1994.*

Version Three:

Great green gobs of greasy, grimy gopher guts,
Marinated monkey meat.
Even though the birdies (?) eat
French-fried eyeballs boiled (?) in a bowl of blood.
I wish I had a spoon.

◆ *Randy, mid-Michigan, who learned it from friends at age twelve or thirteen, 1978-1979. Question marks are informant's own.*

Version Four:

Great big gobs of greasy, grimy gopher guts,
Marinated monkey meat,
Vulture vomit at my feet,
And me without my spoon.

◆ *Jim, St. Patrick's Parochial School, Bedford, New York, ca. 1960s.*

Version Five:

Great green gobs of greasy grimy gopher guts,
Mutilated monkey meat,
Elvis Presley's dirty feet.
Great green gobs of greasy grimy gopher guts,
And me without my spoon.
(spoken) Yum!

◆ *Susan, Ohio, ca. 1970s.*

Version Six:

Great big gobs of ooey gooey gopher guts,
Mutilated monkey meat,
Little bitty birdie feet;
Mix them up with barbecued baby brains,
Then hand me a spoon.

◆ *Gary, Florida, ca. 1960s.*

Version Seven:

Great green gobs of greasy grimy gopher guts,
Mutilated monkey meat,
Little dirty birdy feet,
Vulture vomit hanging from an apple tree,
And me without my spoon!
But I got a straw.

◆ *JoAnn, Louisiana, late 1960s.*

Version Eight:

Great big gobs of greasy, grimy gopher guts,
Mutilated monkey butts,
Chewed-up parakeets.
All this is rolling up and down the streets,
Rolling in a barrel of pus!
I forgot my spoon, so I'll use my straw …
Slurp! Ahhhh ….

◆ *Julie, Natick, Massachusetts, ca. 1975.*

Version Nine:

Great green gobs of greasy, grimy gopher meat,
Mentalated (sic) monkey meat,
(line missing)
French-fried eyeballs floating in a tub of blood—
And I forgot my spoon!
Here's a straw!
Slurp!—Mmmmm, that was good!

◆ *Alan, Birmingham, Alabama, third or fourth grade in the late 1960s.*

Version Ten:

Great green gobs of greasy, grimy gopher meat,

Mutilated monkey meat,
Little birdie chopped-up feet,
All wrapped up in little parts of doggy (kitty) skin,
And I forgot my spoon.
So they gave me horsemeat, sugar on top,
Elephant eyeballs filled with snot,
Lima beans filled with glue;
Eat up! It's good for you!

 Annette, Jacksonville, Florida, age five, "1973ish." The informant adds, "I heard variations of it in Illinois (baby skins instead of dogs or cats, 1976), Tennessee (squirrel meat instead of horsemeat, 1977), southeast Florida, near Fort Lauderdale (gator meat for horsemeat, 1980), Maryland (crab meat instead of horsemeat, brussels sprouts for lima beans, although the lima beans were named by some, 1985).

Version Eleven:

Great green globs of greasy grimy gopher guts,
Mutilated monkey feet,
Chopped-up baby parakeet,
French-fried eyeballs rolling down the dirty street,
And I forgot my spoon.

So give me a sandwich with pus on top,
Monkey vomit and camel snot,
French-friend eyeballs dipped in doo,
Eat it, (name), it's good for you!

 Marla, who knew the first part from her childhood in Queens, New York, ca. late 1970s, and learned the second part in 1986 from nine-year-olds on the bus when she was camp counselor on Long Island.

Version Twelve:

Gobs and gobs of greasy, grimy gopher guts,

Mutilated monkey meat,
Little birdie's dirty feet.
Bowls and bowls of prehistoric porpoise pus,
That's what we served to you.

◆ *Richard, Anne Arundel County, Maryland, ca. 1968-1970.*

Version Thirteen:

Greemy, grisy, gofer (sic) guts,
Attract lots of hungry nuts,
Some with bruises, some with cuts,
All fighting over greemy, grisy, gofer guts.

◆ *Garvey, North Little Rock, age nine, 1994.*

Version Fourteen:

Boys are made of greasy, grimy gopher guts,
Chopped-up parakeet,
Mutilated monkey meat.
Boys are made of French-fried eyeballs.
Oops, I dropped my spoon.

◆ *Lenny, New Jersey, ca. 1970. The informant, who was slightly older than the singers, remembers a group of fifth-grade girls singing it on the school bus, deliberately raising their voices so that the boys could hear them. However, Karen, Fort Worth, Texas, ca. 1967, recalls hearing a very similar boys' version that began "Girls are made of ..."*

Version Fifteen:

Boys are made of ooey-gooey gopher guts,
Chopped-up chicken feed,
Evaporated monkey milk,
All wrapped up in all-purpose porpoise pus,
And I forgot my spoon.

◆ *Janice, Florida, ca. 1960s.*

Version Sixteen:

Great big gobs of greasy, grimy gopher guts,
Chopped-up chicken feet cooked in kerosine,
French-fried eyeballs, swimming in a pool of blood.
That's what I think of you!

◆ *Daniel, Eagle Public School, Eagle, Alaska, second grade, ca. 1978.*

Version Seventeen:

Great green gobs of greasy, grimy gopher guts,
Mutilated monkey brains,
Little pigs on a string,
All wrapped up in
(line missing)
And I forgot my spoon.
(shouted) What's for lunch?

◆ *Laura Ann, Central Jersey, ca. mid-1970s. The informant added that she learned this from her older sister, Suzanne, and that an alternate third line was, "Little pigs soaked in brine."*

Version Eighteen:

Guess what we had at the school cafeteria,
The school cafeteria, the school cafeteria,
Guess what we had at the school cafeteria
For our lunch today.
We had great big gobs of greasy, grimy gopher guts,
Marinated monkey meat,
Candy-coated bumblebees,

Great big gobs of greasy, grimy gopher guts.
Forgot a spoon, had a straw, slurp, slurp!

◆ *K.C., St. Joseph Catholic School, Amarillo, Texas, sixth grade, ca. 1970s. The informant adds, "It is best sung by the entire class (at the top of their lungs) during lunch."*

Version Nineteen:

I woke up one fine morning
And what do you think I saw?
The bedbugs and the cooties
Were having a game of ball.
The score was ten to nothing,
The cooties had the lead;
The bedbugs hit a homer,
And knocked me out of bed.

I went downstairs
And what do you think I saw?
I saw ...
Great green gobs of greasy, grimy gopher guts,
Mutilated monkey meat,
Little dirty birdy feet
(repeat previous three lines as fast as possible)
... and I forgot my spoon!

◆ *Darryl, Philadelphia, Pennsylvania, ca. 1970s.*

Version Twenty:

Greasy, Grimy, Gopher, Guts,
Live in really silly huts,
If you touch them, you might die,
So you'd better wave goodbye!

◆ *Informants, Ben, Peter, and Michael, age eight, Reston Public
School, Reston, Virginia, May, 1994.*[2]

A good many other gross-out rhymes also celebrate the
thought of eating the most unlikely or out-and-out disgusting
substances possible. Sometimes this is done merely because it

Section One: Getting Down to Basics

gives a child the chance to parody an existing rhyme or popular song, but sometimes these are definitely intended to make fun of those occasional bouts of total insecurity and feelings of "everybody hates me:"

Version One:

Nobody likes me, everybody hates me,
Why did I eat those worms?
Long, thin slimy ones,
Short, fat juicy ones,
Itty bitty fuzzy wuzzy worms.

First you bite the heads off,
Then you suck the guts out,
Then you throw the rest away.

Everybody loves me, nobody hates me,
Why did I eat those worms?

◆ *Amy, Cupertino, California, heard as a tenth grader, from her sister, age ten, ca. 1970s.*

Version Two:

Nobody likes me,
Everybody hates me,
Going to the garden to eat some worms.
Big, fat juicy worms,
Small, slimy skinny worms.
The first goes down all right—gulp.
The second slides down just fine—gulp.
The third got stuck in my throat—hack, hack.

◆ *Jessica, Montreal, Quebec, Canada, ca. 1960.*

Version Three:

Nobody likes me, everybody hates me,

I'm gonna go eat worms.
Big ones and little ones,
Ishy guishy squishy ones,
I'm gonna go eat worms.

I'm gonna die,
Everybody cry,
I'm gonna eat some worms.

◆ *Jim, St. Patrick's Parochial School, Bedford, New York, ca.*
1960s.

Version Four:

Nobody loves me, everybody hates me,
Think I'll go eat worms.
Short fat juicy ones, little bitty skinny ones,
Swallow them as they squirm.
Bite their heads off, suck the juice out,
Throw the skins away.
Nobody knows how good we can live on worms three
    times a day.

◆ *Robert, Chevy Chase, Maryland, who learned this from his sister*
at age eight to ten, 1956-1960. A similar version comes from
Cory, Toronto, Ontario, Canada, ca. 1980s; Katie, Northwest
Chicago suburbs, 1955-60, and Meg, Wisconsin, ca. 1950s, con-
tributed partial variations.[3]

Other, even less palatable substances, form the inspiration
for rhymes:

Lincoln, Lincoln, I been thinkin',
What the heck have you been drinkin'?
Looks like water and tastes like wine,
Oh my god, it's turpentine.

◆ *Author Weisskopf, Brooklyn, New York, ca. early 1960s. Also contributed by Alan, ca. 1960s, Florida, and Cat, ca. 1966, New Jersey, who used it as a jump-rope rhyme. Similar versions were contributed by Kathy, Henry Harris Elementary School, Bayonne, New Jersey, ca. mid-1960s; Lois, Lincoln Elementary School, South Bend, Indiana, 1950s; Bruce, Phoenix Central School, Phoenix, New York, late 1950s; Alan, Florida, ca. 1960s—his version begins "Reuben, Reuben"; and Jerri, Doraville, GA, ca. 1970 (who knew a variant first line, "Abraham Lincoln, I've been thinkin' ").*

Little Miss Muffet
Sat on a tuffet
Eating her curds and whey.
Along came a spider
And sat down beside her
And she ate that, too.

◆ Katya, Fairborn, Ohio, ca. 1963.[4]

Both children and adults may find the insect and arachnid families fascinating, but almost no one likes the idea of having an insect turning up on one's body. There is still a problem with head lice in schools, and anyone who lives in a big city knows there is also a problem with unwanted "guests" such as cockroaches or silverfish in apartment houses. But most children's rhymes on the subject of insects paying personal visits concentrate instead on the far less common subject of bedbugs:

Version One:

(to be sung to "The Star-Spangled Banner")

Oo-oh, say can you see
Any bedbugs on me?
If you do, pick a few—

'Cause I got them from you.

◆ *Mary, San Francisco Bay area, California, ca. 1980s.*

Version Two:

Oh say can you see
All the bedbugs on me.
If you do, take a few,
'Cause I got them from you.

Oh say, does that star-spangled
Bedbug yet wave?
O'er the beds of the free
And the bugs of the brave?

◆ *Hank, Benham, Kentucky, ca. 1957 to 1959.*[5]

Children are often genuinely in peril of getting run over by various machines, particularly trains and automobiles. They may even have lost pets to the latter. But the folk process helps blunt the terror of such a fate and turns the horror into something so exaggerated that it becomes funny:

Version One:

(to the tune of "I'm Looking Over a Four-Leafed Clover")

I'm looking over my dead dog Rover
That I ran over with the mower.
One leg is missing,
The other is gone.
The third one is lying all over the lawn.
No need explaining the one remaining,
It's nailed to the kitchen door.
I'm looking over my dead dog Rover
That I ran over with the mower.

◆ *Dori, Minnesota, ca. 1981. A similar variant was collected from Chris, Stiles Pond, Massachusetts, who learned it at age ten in 1979 from a friend, Adam; Jim, Westchester, New York, ca. 1960s.*

Version Two:

I'm looking over my dead dog Rover
That I overlooked before.
One leg is broken, the other is lame.
I ran him over with my Cocoa Puff Train.
No need explaining the legs remaining,
They're lying there on the floor.
I'm looking over my dead dog Rover
That I overran before.

◆ *Author Sherman, New York City, ca. 1970s; similar versions were collected from Darryl, Philadelphia, Pennsylvania, ca. 1970s; Janice, Florida, ca. 1960s; Jim, Westchester, New York, ca. 1960s, and Greg, Connecticut, ca. late 1960s.*

Version Three:

I'm looking over my dead dog Rover
Lying on the bathroom floor.
One leg is broken,
The other one's lame,
The third got run over
By my 'lectric train.
There's no use explaining,
The one remaining
Is stuck in the bathroom door.
I'm looking over my dead dog Rover,
Lying on the bathroom floor.

(spoken)
Same song, second verse,

A little bit faster and a whole lot worse.
(Sing the whole song again really fast.)

◆ *Nancy, day camp at Johns Hopkins' Hospital Center, Washington, D.C., ca. 1968-69.*[6]

A little anthropomorphism lends drama to the end of less lovable entities than Rover:

Version One:

Peanut sitting on a track,
Heart was all a-flutter.
Train came screeching down the track.
Toot! Toot!
Peanut Butter.

◆ *Dick, Washington, D.C. suburbs, mid-1960s.*

Version Two:

Ooey-Gooey was a worm,
Ooey-Gooey liked to squirm.
Ooey-Gooey sat on the railroad tracks.
TOOT, TOOT!
(in tone of extreme disgust) OOEY-GOOEY!

◆ *Judy, who learned it from her father, Maine, ca. 1960. A similar version was collected from Kathy, learned from her mother, Bayonne, New Jersey, ca. 1960.*

Version Three:

Ooey-Gooey was a worm.
Ooey-Gooey loved to squirm.
Ooey-Gooey saw a truck.
Ooey-Gooey forgot to duck.

"Ooey-Gooey!"

◆ *Tom, Portland, Oregon, ca. early 1960s.*[7]

Gross-outs can range from the dramatic deaths of squashed peanuts and critters to yet another graphically fascinating premise: contaminated food—particularly that contaminated by human waste:

Gramma's in the cellar.
Lord, can't you smell 'er,
Cookin' biscuits on that darned old dirty stove.
In her eye there is some matter
That keeps dripping in the batter.
(repeat above two lines)
And the *(snort)* keeps dripping down 'er nose.
Down her nose (down her nose),
Down her nose (down her nose),
And the *(snort)* keeps dripping down her nose.

◆ *Elizabeth, Camp Reily, Harrisburg, Pennsylvania, ca. 1975.*[8]

And, of course, there's always the minor but very possible gross-out subject of wearing clothing a bit too often between washings:

(to the tune of the folk song, "White Wings")

Black socks, they never get dirty,
The longer you wear them, the stiffer they get.
Black socks, I think about laundry,
But something inside me says don't send them yet.

◆ *Katie, Northwest Chicago suburbs, ca. 1955-1960.*

This one starts out sounding like a dirty rhyme, then ends with a gross-out zinger in the last line:

There's a place in France
Where the naked ladies dance,
But the men don't care
'Cause they chew their underwear.

◆ *Kari, Minnesota, mid-1970s.* 9

CHAPTER TWO:

IN THE BEGINNING: SEX, PREGNANCY, AND BIRTH

A good many of the rhymes we collected both from adults and children dealt, sometimes quite blatantly, with sex—not a surprising fact since this subject is one of endless fascination to humanity. Informants eight years old or younger didn't always understand all—or sometimes any—of the implications in the rhymes they sang or chanted by rote. Slightly older informants (those children old enough to think they understood what the rhymes were actually saying, as well as those who actually did) tended to accompany their recitations with a good deal of giggling. The reaction of teenagers was usually a mix of laughter and embarrassment at saying such rhymes in front of adults and, in the case of boys, in front of adult women. We assume that the adult informants, who also often broke into giggles, knew what they were reciting.

Often children's folk rhymes, sexual or otherwise, take the form of rhythmic chants, rather than actual songs, repeated during jumping-rope or hand-clapping games, or counting-out rhymes.

Following are two variants on one very popular and widespread jump-rope rhyme:

Version One:

Cinderella, dressed in yellow,
Went upstairs to kiss her fellow;
Made a mistake and kissed a snake
How many doctors will it take?
(counts to thirteen and adds, "and so on.")

◆ *Casey, Park Hill Elementary School, North Little Rock, Arkansas,*
age ten, 1994. Almost identical versions were contributed by
Kristina and Marquita, also ten and from the same school.

Version Two:

Cinderella, dressed in yella,
Went upstairs to kiss her fella.
By mistake she kissed a snake.
Cinderella, dressed in yella.

◆ *Laura, Dogwood, Virginia, age eight, 1994. The "yella" and*
"fella" spelling was quite deliberate; the "punchline" involving
the doctor wasn't known to the informant.[1]

Another, more titillating form of rhyme popular among
children in the United States is the one in which the speaker
seems inevitably headed towards dirty words, only to escape
just in the nick of time. While these rhymes aren't restricted
primarily to the United States and have a long European ances-
try that dates back far before the founding of this country, one
very popular version that is predominantly American follows:

Version One:

Ms. Lucy had a steamboat, the steamboat had a bell.
Ms. Lucy went to heaven and the steamboat went to ...
Hello operator, please give me number nine,
And if you disconnect me I will chop off your ...

Behind the refrigerator, there was a piece of glass.
Ms. Lucy sat upon it and it went right up her ...
Ask me no more questions, I'll tell you no more lies.
The boys are in the bathroom pulling down their ...
Flies are in the meadow, the meadow's in the park.
The boys and girls are kissing in the
D.A.R.K. D.A.R.K. D.A.R.K. dark dark dark.
The dark is like a movie, a movie's like a show
A show is like a TV set, and that is all I know ...
I know I know my mother, I know I know my pop.
I know I know my sister with the 18-hour
18-hour 18-hour bra bra bra.

◆ *Jessica, who learned the rhyme at camp in New York state, age
seven or eight, circa 1984; also known in an almost identical version by Mischel, Mamaroneck, New York, age eight, 1994.*[2]

Version Two:

Helen had a tugboat, Helen had a bell.
Every time she rang it, the tugboat went to ...
Hello operator, give me number nine,
And if she doesn't answer, give me back my dime.
Behind the refrigerator was a piece of glass.
Helen slipped on it and broke her little ...
Ask me no more questions, I'll tell you no more lies.
That's what Helen told me the night before she died.

◆ *Lindalee, Brownie day camp, Manitowoc, Wisconsin, ca. 1959-60.*

Version Three:

... Ask me no more questions, I'll tell you no more lies.
The boys are in the basement, pulling down their ...
Flies in the buttermilk shoo-fly-shoo,
Flies in the buttermilk shoo-fly-shoo,
Flies in the buttermilk shoo-fly-shoo,

And that's the story of Lulu.

◆ *Tina, P.S. 95, Bronx, New York, late 1950s.*[3]

Version Four:

Johnny had a steamboat, steamboat had a bell,
Johnny got some dynamite and blasted it to ...
Hello operator, give me number nine,
And if the line is busy, I'll kick you in the ...
Behind the Iron Curtain was a little piece of glass.
Johnny fell upon it and hurt his little ...
Ask a silly question, and the answer is a lie!

◆ *Debbie, ca. twelve years old, 1960s. Informant adds, "I learned (this) in Germany, of all places! Amazing how close cousins of these rhymes can transcend time and distance, isn't it? Quality survives?"*[4]

Version Five:

Hello, operator. Give me number nine.
If you disconnect me, I'll kick you in the ...
'*Hind* the fridgerator, there was a piece of glass.
Miss Suzy sat upon, and cut her little ...
Ask me no more questions, I'll tell you no more lies.
The cows are in the pasture, making chocolate pies.

◆ *Caroline, Huntsville, Alabama, early 1970s.*

There are many other forms of rhyme popular in this country that play the game of just managing to avoid the dirty words. Three such rhymes follow:

Version One:

Suzanne was a lady with plenty of class,
Who drove the boys mad when she wiggled her ...

Eyes at the fellows as girls sometimes do,
To make it quite plain she was ready to ...
Go for a walk or a stroll through the grass,
And then hurry home for a nice piece of ...
Ice cream and cake and a piece of roast duck,
And after each meal she was ready to ...
Go for a walk or a stroll on the dock
With any young man with a sizeable ...
Roll of green bills and a pretty good front
And if he talked fast she would show him her ...
Little pet dog that was subject to fits
And maybe let him grab ahold of her ...
Little white hand with a movement so quick,
Then she'd lean over and tickle his ...
Chin while she showed what she learned in France,
And ask the poor fellow to take off his ...
Coat while she sang "Off the Mandalay Shore."
For whatever she was, Susanne was no bore.

◆ *Jim, Bedford, New York, 1970s.*[5]

Version Two:

Mikey and Ikey were playing the ditch
When Mikey told Ikey you dirty son of a ...
Bring down the children so they learn to play with
Sticks so when they get older they learn to play with ...
Dickie had a brother,
They named him Tiny Tim.
They put him in the piss pot,
To see if he could swim.
He swam to the bottom,
He swam to the top.
And when he came up he was playing with his ...
Cocktail ginger ale, five cents a glass.
If you don't believe me,
I'll kick you straight up your ...

Ask me no more questions,
I'll tell you no more lies.
Still don't believe me,
I'll kick you straight in your eye.

◆ *Candy, Bronx, New York, 1970s.*[6]

Version Three:

I shot an arrow in the air,
Where it lands, I know not where.
From my maiden I heard a grunt,
Though it hit her in the ...
Country boy, country boy, sitting on a rock,
Gopher came along and bit off his ...
Cocktail, cocktail, five cents a glass,
If you don't like it, shove it up your ...
Ask me no questions, I'll tell you no lies.
If you get hit by a bucket of sh__,
Be sure to close your eyes.

◆ *Barrie, Wisconsin, age eight or nine, ca. 1959.*[7]

Every now and then, one of these deceptive, not-quite
dirty rhymes, instead of slipping in a "taboo" word in the middle of things, concludes with a startling twist:

There once was a farmer who took a young miss
In back of the barnyard and gave her a ...
Lecture on horses and chickens and eggs
He told her that she had such beautiful ...
Manners, a girl of sweet charms,
A girl that he wanted to take in his ...
Washing and ironing and then if she did,
They could get married and raise lots of ...

Sweet violets, sweeter than the roses.
Covered all over from head to toe
Covered all over in ...
Sh___.

♦ *Jeanne, first heard in North Carolina, ca. 1970s. The informant adds, "The good version that you sing around your parents just ends with 'sweet violets.' When you're singing it as kids, you sort of pause there, then say 'sh___.' " A similar version without the "zinger" ending was collected from Debbie, New York, ca. 1970s. The informant's comment: "A rather fascinating social document, on several levels." 8*

In the folk-rhyme community, Lulu of steamboat fame finds a close cousin in the much more promiscuous Rosie, star of some blatantly bawdy rhymes sung or chanted, often to accompany hand-clapping or jump-rope games by children who may or may not understand the implications, but who know these are definitely not songs to be sung before adults. A particularly complete version follows:

Bang bang Rosie,
Rosie's gone away.
She's going to have a baby,
That's why she's gone away.
Rosie had two boyfriends,
Both of them were rich.
One was the son of a lawyer
The other's the son of a—
Bang bang Rosie,
Rosie's gone away.
She's going to have a baby,
That's why she's gone away.
Rosie had a rooster,
Rosie had a duck.
She put them both together

To see if they could—
Bang bang Rosie,
Rosie's gone away.
She's going to have a baby,
That's why she's gone away.
In the refrigerator
There is a piece of glass,
And if you do not like it
You can stick it up your—

◆ *Janni Lee, Long Island, New York, ca. 1980. A similar, shortened
version is known to author Weisskopf, 1975, Brooklyn, New York.*[9]
*Informant Janni Lee added, "[It was] taught to me by a cousin who
had learned it from my mom (much to the dismay of her mom)."*

Janni Lee continued with the following variant:

Version One:

Rosie had a baby.
She named him Tiny Tim.
She put him in the toilet
To see if he could swim.
He swam to the bottom,
He swam to the top,
And when he nearly drownded (sic),
She grabbed him by the
Cocktail, gin ginger ale.[10]

Version Two:

Miss Suzy had a baby.
She named it Tiny Tim.
She put him in the bathtub
To see if he could swim.
He drank up all the water
He ate up all the soap,

And now he's home sick in
Bed with bubbles in his throat!
BURP!

◆ *Katie, Sunrise Valley Elementary School, Reston, Virginia, age eight, 1994. She recalls learning it from friends in North Carolina.*[11]

Version Three:

Miss Suzy had a baby.
She named him Tiny Tim.
She put in the bathtub
To see if he could swim.
He drank up all the water.
He ate a bar of soap.
He tried to eat the bathtub,
But it wouldn't go down his throat.
Miss Suzy called the doctor.
Miss Suzy called the nurse.
Miss Suzy called the lady
With the alligator purse.
"Mumps," said the doctor.
"Measles," said the nurse.
"Nothing," said the lady with the alligator purse!

◆ *Caroline, Huntsville, Alabama, 1970s; similarly, Kate, 1960s, Arizona, who adds that this rhyme is still "contemporary in southern Arizona."*[12]

Version Four:

Molly had a bear named Tiny Tim.
Put him in the water to see if he could swim.
He drank up all the water,
He ate all the soap,
He died the next morning with a bubble in his throat.

◆ *Diana, Reston, Virginia, age eight, 1994.*[13]

Not all examples of this category of folk rhyme are so graphic or, for that matter, so fatal to the characters. A much more innocuous sexual rhyme is also very popular with children across the country:

Version One:

Helen and Ronnie up in a tree,
K-I-S-S-I-N-G.
First comes love, then comes marriage,
Then comes Ronnie with a baby carriage.

◆ *Judith, Maine, seventh grade, 1967. She notes, "These were the seventh-grade class lovebirds."*[14]

Version Two:

Two little lovers, sitting in a tree,
K-I-S-S-I-N-G.
First comes love, then comes marriage,
Then two little babies in a baby carriage.

◆ *Daniel, Eagle Public School, Eagle, Alaska, ca. 1978.*[15]

Version Three:

(Boy's name) and (Girl's name) sitting in a tree,
K-I-S-S-I-N-G.
First comes love, then comes marriage, then comes
    (name) in a baby carriage,
Suckin' their thumbs, wettin' their pants, doin' the naked
    hula dance.

◆ *Katherine, New Hampshire, age eleven, 1994. Also known to Michelle, age six, 1994, Bronx, New York. Michelle's rhyme, otherwise the same as the above, changed the last line to "the Hula Hula Dance."*[16]

Version Four:

(Girl) and (boy) sitting in a tree,
K-I-S-S-I-N-G.
First comes love, then comes marriage,
Then comes (boy) in the baby carriage.
That's not it and that's not all,
Then comes the baby drinking alcohol.

 Michelle, Bronx, New York, six years old, 1994. The informant added that this rhyme was "for boys." Lorelei, seven years old, 1994, Glen Ellyn, Illinois, knew a similar version that omitted boy as the baby and changed the last line to a less startling but more frenetic, "The baby is dancing up the wall."[17]

❖

Trees aren't the only places boys and girls get together:

(Girl) and (boy) sitting in a car.
Are they naked? Yes they are.
(Girl) falls out,
(Boy) saves her life.
Now I pronounce you
Man and wife.

 Michelle, Bronx, New York, six years old, 1994.[18]

❖

Sex sometimes results in pregnancy and birth. While children may not always have been told or have figured out for themselves the connection between sex and birth, they have no intention of avoiding rhymes about the latter fascinating subject, either! One very popular jump-rope rhyme found all over the United States follows:

Judge, fudge, call the judge.
Going to have a newborn baby.
Wrap it up in tissue paper,

Send it down the elevator,
A boy, a girl, twin or triplets ...

◆ *Informants: Cherell, Kristina, and several other ten-year-old girls in the Park Hill Elementary School, North Little Rock, 1994, all of whom had only minor variations on the basic theme. The informants' comment: "It's a jump-rope rhyme." The ending is repeated till the jumper is "out." A similar version is collected from Laura, Dogwood, Virginia, age eight, 1994.*[19]

Some of the facts of life can be transmitted from one child to another (in this case, and in most cases, from one girl to another) in rhymes of warning. The following is to be sung to the tune of "My Darling Clementine":

(Woman) take this good advice from me,
Don't let (man) get an inch above your knee.
He will tell you that he loves you,
and will fill your heart with joy,
Then he'll leave you brokenhearted
with a bouncing baby boy.

◆ *Claire, who heard this song at camp in New York State in the late 1960s.*[20]

Another cautionary rhyme parodies a famous song from the Lerner and Loewe musical, *My Fair Lady:*

I should have danced all night,
I should have danced all night,
But still I asked for more!
I should have spread my wings,
But I spread other things
I've never spread before.
I really know that it was so excited

I also know just what took flight!
And I do know that he
Did what he done to me!
I should have danced, danced, danced all night!

◆ *Diane, ca. 1969 or 1970. "A friend of mine and I did this at an assembly when we were in eighth or ninth grade. We were supposed to be singing the real words, of course. Was our Music Teacher ever P.O.'d ... Not to mention the principal (and our parents!)."*[21]

Another series of rhymes takes the situation a little further. An example follows:

Ta-da-da-boom-di-ay,
How did I get this way?
Was it the boy next door?
He pushed me on the floor.

He lifted up my skirt,
He said it wouldn't hurt.
And while my eyes did stare,
He pulled down my underwear.

And right before my eyes,
I saw my tummy rise.

◆ *Robin, Dartmouth, Massachusetts, 1970s. The informant couldn't remember the couplet following "underwear."*[22]

And sometimes the connections between sex, pregnancy, and birth are made almost clinically clear:

(to the tune of "The Colonel Bogey March")

Herman, look what you've done to me!

Herman, I think it's pregnancy!
Herman, you put your sperm in,
And now it's Herman, and Sherman, and me!

◆ *Jessica, who learned it at a slumber party at age ten, New York City, New York, 1987.*[23]

As children go through puberty, their rhymes, understandably, become more sexually explicit, and often take the form of taunts or outright insults against other teenagers. The following is a "boys only" rhyme, to be chanted at a foe:

(Name) is a friend of mine,
He will blow you anytime,
For a nickel or a dime,
Fifteen cents if overtime.

Now he has a union card,
He will blow you twice as hard,
For a nickel or a dime,
Fifteen cents if overtime.

◆ *"M.J.", Hammond, Indiana, teenaged boy, 1960s.*[24]

Girls have their taunts and teasing songs, too, often aimed at boys. These rhymes tend to be less openly explicit but no less sexual in nature. The following would be chanted by a girl to a group of boys while she slowly hitched up her skirt:

One, two, three, four,
Hitch it up a little more.
Five, six, seven, eight,
Sorry, boys, coffee break.

◆ *Jim, an adult from New Hampshire, who was told this by his daughter, who was in sixth grade in 1992. The informant added, "The last line comes just before what might be termed the 'moment of truth,' at which point the skirt is dropped."* [25]

The following rhymes express a new slant on the sexual theme: they reveal children's budding awareness that just as there are differences in physical appearance, so there are differences in sexual orientation. Sometimes this awareness can be unfavorably tainted by adult prejudices:

Version One:

(to be sung to the tune of "Pop Goes the Weasel")

We don't go out with the boys anymore,
We don't intend to marry,
We go with the girls in our block,
Whee! I'm a fairy.

◆ *Caryl, Rockford, Illinois, ca. 1952. The informant added, "On Thursday you couldn't wear yellow and green or you'd be saying you were a fairy."* [26]

Version Two:

(to be sung to the tune of "Pop Goes the Weasel")

You don't go out with boys anymore,
You don't like Elvis Presley.
You sit in the corner and play with yourself.
Oops, you're a lesie!

◆ *Sue, Brooklyn, New York, ca. 1967-75.* [27]

More modern rhymes on this theme tend to be a little more blunt, but also a little more tolerant of differences:

Version One:

I love you, you love me,
Homosexuality,
You may think we're ordinary friends,
But we're really lesbians.

◆ *Katherine, age eleven, 1994, New Hampshire. The informant added a variant third line: "We're not what we seem to be." Similarly Caroline, Huntsville, Alabama, early 1970s.*

Version Two:

I hate you, you hate me,
Homosexuality.
With a slap on the butt
And a kiss from me to you,
Won't you say you're horny too?

◆ *Josh, age twelve, 1994, Wisconsin.*[28]

Of course, one of the fascinating aspects about the dawning of sexual feelings is learning about the differences in male and female anatomy. This is a subject for much giggling among children of all ages, and the creation of rhymes such as the following:

Version One:

Oh, they don't wear pants
When they hula hula dance,
And the girls get in line,
And they wiggle their behinds,
And when the grass falls down
There's a riot in the town.

◆ *Tina, Bronx, New York, ca. 1950s.*[29]

Version Two:

On the sunny side of France,
They don't wear pants.
They do wear grass
To cover up their ...
On the sunny side of France.

◆ *Vera, Cambridge, Massachusetts, ca. 1950s.* [30]

Version Three:

Charlie Chaplin went to France
To teach the girls the hoola hoola dance.
First on the heels, then on the toes.
Do the splits, and around she goes.
Salute to the captain, now to the queen.
Turn your back on the dirty submarine.

◆ *Rod, Modesto, California, 1975.*[31]

Version Four:

There's a place in France
Where the naked ladies dance.
There's a hole in the wall
Where the boys can see it all.

◆ *Colleen, Hastings, New York, age eleven, 1994. The informant, who first heard this song when she was seven, stated that this was sung mainly by boys, but added (with warnings that it was a very "dirty" song) a version sung (in retaliation?) by girls:*

Version Five:

There's a place in Venus
Where the men show their penis.
There's a hole in the wall
Where the girls can see it all.[32]

Section One: Getting Down to Basics

Version Six:

There's a place in France
Where the naked ladies dance.
There's a hole in the wall
Where the men can see it all.
But the men don't care
'Cause they're in their underwear.

♦ *Kathryn, age seven, ca. 1990s, who learned it from Elizabeth, age seven, who learned it from Kara, age nine, who learned it from Katy, age eight, who learned it from television (!).*[33]

Boys also come in for their share of anatomical revelations, as in the following insult rhyme:

Here comes Batman,
Swinging on a rubber band,
Stronger than Superman.
Here comes King Kong,
Beating on his ding dong.

♦ *William, who heard it at age eight at St. Matthew's School, Yonkers, New York, age eleven, 1994. The informant added that this rhyme would be chanted at the boy being insulted. He was embarrassed at saying such a rhyme in front of a woman, and the ending was almost lost in nervous laughter.*[34]

These anatomical rhymes can be used not only as insults but as slightly surreal counting-out rhymes:

Tarzan swings,
Tarzan falls,
Tarzan breaks his
Big, fat balls.

♦ *Colleen, age eleven, 1994, who learned it from her next door neighbor, Michael, in Hastings, New York, when she was nine. The recitation was within hearing range of two eleven-year-old boys, and involved much embarrassed giggling from all three.*[35]

In the next rhyme, very popular in one form or another across the country, there is more boasting than embarrassment:

> Do your balls hang low?
> Do they wobble to and fro?
> Can you tie them in a knot?
> Can you tie them in a bow?
> Can you throw them over your shoulder
> Like a constipated soldier?
> Do your balls hang low?

◆ *George, who learned it in high school at age fourteen or fifteen, ca. 1970s, in Connecticut.*[36]

But there is more to male puberty than sexual boasting or pride; there is also the fear of sexual injury, although it is almost never voiced aloud other than in mocking songs like the following:

> Adam and Eve, sittin' on a rock,
> She was shaving Adam's cock.
> Gonna tie my pecker to a tree, to a tree,
> Gonna tie my pecker to a tree.
> The razor slipped, the razor flew,
> It cut Adam's cock in two.
> Gonna tie my pecker to a tree, to a tree,
> Gonna tie my pecker to a tree.

◆ *Gary, who learned it from his "city" cousin in Burlington, Iowa, in the mid-1950s. The informant added that it was to be sung to a Country and Western tune, although he couldn't remember the title.*[37]

Whatever the formal sexual education or informal guessing and experimentation, by the time of puberty, children have at least a rudimentary grasp of the facts of life, and sometimes, although adults try to deny it, a fairly good idea of how the whole process works:

> One and one are two,
> Two and two are four,
> If the bed collapses,
> Do it on the floor.

◆ *Sharon, Massachusetts, age thirteen, 1994.*[38]

Version One:

> A boy's occupation
> Is to stick his preparation
> Into a girl's separation
> To increase the population
> Of the younger generation.
> Do you want a demonstration?

◆ *Lisa, P.S. 90, Bronx, New York, a sixth grader in 1966.*[39]

Version Two:

> When boy mates girl
> On the floor, floor, floor,
> He sticks his information
> In the girl's communication
> To increase the population
> Of the future generation.
> Do you want a demonstration?

◆ *"D.B.," California, who learned it in eighth grade, ca. 1972.*[40]

Version Three:

The boy's preoccupation
Is to put his boneration
In a girl's separation
To increase the population
Of the younger generation.
If you want a demonstration,
Lie down, sucker.

◆ *A sixth-grade girl from New Hampshire in 1992 "who wishes to remain anonymous." The informant adds, "It's popular among the seventh-grade boys."*[41]

Version Four:

Sex, sex, sex
Is the law, law, law.
When a guy gets a girl
On the floor, floor, floor,
He sticks his information
In the girl's communication
Which increases the population
Of the younger generation.
Would you like a little demonstration?

◆ *Colleen, Hastings, New York, age eleven, 1994. The informant prefaced her recitation with a warning that this rhyme was "really, really bad," and added with distaste that she was nine when an eleven-year-old male neighbor told it to her.*[42] *Sue, Brooklyn, New York, 1980s. knew a version ending "If you want a demonstration,/ Ask the Board of Education.*[43]

CHAPTER THREE:

BODILY FUNCTIONS, ILLNESS, AND DEATH

After the subjects of sex, pregnancy, and birth, some of the most fascinating topics for children—and the most taboo for adults—are those dealing with normal bodily functions, especially anything that drips or oozes, and particularly those subjects "not meant for polite company," such as defecation and urination, functions that a good many adults prefer not to acknowledge, let alone discuss.

Just as fascinating to children, who are, after all, trying their best to figure out the world about them, are the equally taboo topics of what happens when the bodily system breaks down, whether through illness or death. It's pretty terrifying for both children and adults to think about what happens to the body in mortal illness and after death. Humans can't stop death, can't stop being biological constructs like other animals, but we don't have to ignore it: we can have dignity in death. Or we can go the other way and revel in its gory details.

But while many adults try to avoid the subject altogether, children are fascinated and diminish their fear by making fun of it, and by deliberately coming up with the most "gross" rhymes they can imagine. "Gross-outs," are incredibly popular among children of all ages and have been around in one form or another for centuries. The rhymes focus on the disgusting, the corporeal rather than mortality or the hereafter. Gross-outs have the added advantage of revolting any adults within range and eliciting from other children that most satisfying of reactions, "Eeeeuuuuwwww!"[1]

BODILY FUNCTIONS

How the body works is a fascinating subject for children and adults alike. But for adults, only some of the body's functions are considered mentionable in proper society. There are very few children's rhymes about those functions considered permissible in polite company, such as yawning or sneezing; after all, there's no thrill of violating a taboo in reciting such innocuous rhymes, nor is there any tantalizing edge of mystery. But as soon as a bodily function is declared taboo by adults, children begin inventing their rhymes.

Belching (or, as children are usually taught to call it, burping), while hardly considered a polite activity, isn't quite a taboo subject, either—it's something that can happen to anyone and is usually greeted with embarrassment and apology rather than horrified shock. As a result, children create very few rhymes about it. The following is an exception:

> Please forgive my being rude,
> It was not me, it was my food.
> It got so lonely down below,
> It just came up to say hello.

◆ *Jason, Queens, New York, age eighteen, 1994.*[2]

Another fact of life that isn't exactly unacceptable but which adults try to deny is that the human body has definite odors. Adults attempt to mask these natural odors with various deodorants. While we did not encounter any rhymes about other body odors, children are quite open about such things as smelly feet:

(to be sung to the tune of "Dixie")

Version One:

I wish I was in the land of cotton,
Your feet stink, and mine are rotten.

◆ *W.C., "the South," 1970s.*

Version Two:

I wish I was in the land of cotton,
My feet smell, but yours are rotten.
Look away (pee-you!); Look away (pee-you!);
Look away (pee-you!) Dixieland.

◆ *Mitch, boy scout camp, Suffolk, Long Island, New York, 1972. The informant added, "The pee-yous [are] said while turning the head away and holding one's nose, as though you smelled something bad."[3]*

(to be sung to the tune of "My Bonnie Lies Over the Ocean")

Last night as I lay on my pillow,
Last night as I lay on my bed,
My feet stuck out of the window,
When I woke up, my neighbors were dead.

◆ *Katie, Northwest Chicago suburbs, ca. 1955-1960.[4]*

Slightly worse on the scale of unacceptable bodily functions is the euphemistically named "breaking wind." The very fact that it has been given such a genteel euphemism emphasizes its unsuitability as a topic of polite adult conversation. Children, of course, are not so prim:

Version One:

Beans, beans, they're good for your heart,
The more you eat, the more you fart.
The more you fart, the better you feel,
So eat your beans at every meal.

◆ *Marla, who learned it at a New York City area camp between 1980 and 1983. Also known to author Weisskopf and to author Sherman, who probably first heard it in the 1970s in New York City. A similar version was collected from Lawrence, who heard in the early 1980s on Long Island, and Cliff, who learned it at five or six in Elkton, Maryland, ca. 1952. Cliff's variation ended with "So eat baked beans with every meal."*

Version Two:

Beans, beans, the musical fruit,
The more you eat, the more you toot.
The more you toot, the better you feel,
Eat beans, beans, at every meal!

◆ *Mary, San Francisco Bay area, California, 1980s.   The first two lines were also contributed by Lisa, Bronx, New York, sixth grade, 1966. This informant also knew "Beans, beans, good for your heart."*

Version Three:

Beans, beans, the musical fruit,
The more you toot the more you wish.
That's why beans are my favorite dish.

◆ *Tappan, Florida, mid-1960s.*

Version Four:

Beans, beans, the musical fruit,
Down yer leg and into your boot.

◆ *David, Renfrew, Ontario, age ten in 1964. The informant added that he had learned the rhyme "from my crazy cousin, Eddie."*[5]

Gene, Gene made a machine,
Joe, Joe made it go,
Frank, Frank turned a crank,
Art, Art let out a fart
and blew it all apart.

◆ *Gary, age six, 1963, South Dakota. An almost identical version, changing Gene to Jean, was contributed by Daniel, who learned it in school between 1974-1980, in Eagle, Alaska; and Mary, 1980s, San Francisco, California, the last line of whose was "Art, Art, let out a fart, and blew the whole damn thing apart."*

I was rolling down the highway,
Highway Forty-Four,
When (name) blew a big one
That blew me out the door.
The windows were all broken,
The car just fell apart.
And all because of (name's)
SUPERSONIC FART!

◆ *Lois, Glen Ellyn, Illinois, 1994, who learned it in 1991 from Christine, her eight-year-old daughter, who in turn learned it from her friend Katie. The informant adds that the rhyme generally ends with the children collapsing into giggles and that the name of the child being insulted is usually a boy, "Most often the singer's older brother."*

(to the tune of "Row, Row, Row Your Boat")

Row, row, row your boat,
Gently down the stream,
Putt, putt, putt, putt,

We're out of gasoline.

◆ *Jim, Our Lady of Good Council Academy, Bedford, New York, late 1950s.*

Fatty and Skinny went to bed.
Fatty rolled over and Skinny was dead.
Mama called the doctor, and the doctor said,
"One more fart and we'll all be dead."

◆ *Rod, Linwood, California, age eight in the early 1960s. Also known to author Weisskopf, from Brooklyn, New York, ca. late 1960s, where the last line is spoken in black dialect.*[6]

Even more taboo bodily functions in adult society are defecation and urination—and, of course, children have come up with rhymes to deal with those familiar functions too. The subject of incontinence is a familiar problem for many a young child, and the embarrassment surrounding an "accident" has been acknowledged and turned into humor in rhymes such as the following:

Version One:

(to be sung to the tune of "How Dry I Am")

How dry I am,
How wet I'll be,
If I don't find
A place to pee.

◆ *Claudette, North Dakota, mid-1960s.*

Version Two:

How dry I am,
How wet I'll be

If I don't find,
The bathroom key.

I found the key,
I lost the door,
I'll have to do
It on the floor.

◆ Mitch, *boy scout camp, Suffolk, Long Island, New York, 1972.*

Version Three:

How dry I am,
How wet I'll be,
If I don't find
The bathroom key.

I found the key,
But where's the door?
I found the door,
It's on the floor!

◆ *Yvonne, Detroit, Michigan, late 1960s. A similar version is known by author Weisskopf, Brooklyn, New York, 1970s, and Marla, Queens, New York, ca. 1980-1983. The first stanza was also contributed by Claudette, North Dakota, 1960s.*

Version Four:

How dry I am ...
How wet I'll be ...
If I don't find ...
The bathroom key.

It's too late now.
It's on the floor.
My Playtex pants
Will hold no more,
WILL HOLD NO MORE!

◆ *Susan, Youngstown, Ohio, 1960s. Also, Amy, Santa Clara, California, in her early teens in 1964.*[7]

When I was a wee-wee tot
My mama put me on the wee pot.
She put me on the wee-wee pot,
To see if I could wee or not.

When she found that I could not,
She took me off the wee-wee pot.
She put me on my wee-wee cot,
And there I wee-wee'd quite a lot.

◆ *Adam, who learned it at camp in Honesdale, Pennsylvania, late 1960s.*[8]

As children grow older, their problems (and fascination) with urination remain. The following is a cautionary rhyme, obviously for boys:

If the hose is short,
And the pressure's weak,
Don't stand far away,
Or you'll soak your feet.

◆ *Chad, who heard it from John, who heard it in Texas ca. 1974.*[9]

Girls, of course, don't have the same anatomical difficulties as boys. But girls can be the subject of rhymes about urination—even if those rhymes are usually invented by boys:

Did you ever see Sally make water?
She pisses a beautiful stream.
She can piss a mile and a quarter,
She's a regular pissing machine.

◆ *Jerry, upstate New York, 1940s or 1950s. Tom, Florida, 1960s, offered a different last line: You can't see her ass for the steam.*[10]

Listen, my children, and you shall hear
Of the midnight run of Paul Revere.
Out of the bed and onto the floor
Fifty-yard dash to the bathroom door.
Hasten, Jason, get the basin.
Plop, plop.
Too late. Get the mop.

◆ *Lawrence, Long Island, New York, early 1980s.*[11]

Defecation receives its fair share of notice in children's rhymes as well, including this instructional verse that discusses both urination and defecation. The words are innocuous, but the gestures that go with it make the subject matter clear:

Milk, milk
Lemonade.
Round the corner
Fudge is made.

◆ *Caroline, Huntsville, Alabama, early 1970s: "As you say it, you point first to the chests, the groin area, then the rear."*

Then there is pseudo-historical verse that makes one feel superior about one's own advanced time:

In days of old, when knights were bold,
And toilets weren't invented,
They did their load upon the road
And walked away contented.

◆ *Evelyn, Bronx, New York, ca. early 1950s.*

But by far the most popular subject for verses about defecation was the common and uncomfortable problem of diarrhea:

(to be sung to the tune of the Beatles' "Yesterday")

Yesterday,
Diarrhea seemed so far away ...
Now the toilet is so full of clay ...
Suddenly,
I'm not half the man I used to be ...
That's about how much came out of me ...

◆ *John, Michigan, 1960s. The informant could, possibly as a result of adult self-censorship, remember only part of the rhyme.*

Diarrhea, diarrhea.
Got some on my finger,
So I wiped it on the wall.
Diarrhea, diarrhea.

◆ *Rod, Stockton, California, who was a teenager in the early 1980s. The informant added that there was more to this rhyme, but could only recall this stanza.*

Version One:

Diarrhea
(Raspberry), (Raspberry)
Diarrhea
(Raspberry), (Raspberry)
It isn't very funny;
It's really dark and runny.
Diarrhea
(Raspberry), (Raspberry)
Diarrhea

(Raspberry), (Raspberry).

◆ *Claudette, North Dakota, mid-1960s. The informant adds, "The raspberries must be thoroughly wet and disgusting." Also contributed by Laura Ann, central New Jersey, ca. mid-1970s.*

Version Two:

Diarrhea—Thpht! Thpht!
Diarrhea—Thpht! Thpht!
Some people say it's funny,
But it's really, really yummy!
Diarrhea—Thpht! Thpht!
Diarrhea—Thpht! Thpht!

Diarrhea—Thpht! Thpht!
Diarrhea—Thpht! Thpht!
Some people say it's gross,
But it's really great on toast!
Diarrhea—Thpht! Thpht!
Diarrhea—Thpht! Thpht!

◆ *John, at Catholic elementary school, Baton Rouge, Louisiana, ca. 1976. The informant adds, "There were more verses, but these are all I can remember, thank God!"*[12]

Regurgitation is another popular subject of children's rhymes since it, too, is avoided in polite adult conversation, and it happens all too frequently to children:

(to be sung to the tune of the "I'm a Toys 'R' Us Kid" jingle, whicH is to the tune of "I Don't Wanna Grow Up" from the musical Peter Pan.*)*

I don't wanna throw up,
But I already did.
I made it to the toilet,

But I forgot about the lid.

◆ *Jenna, Winnipeg, Canada, age unknown, ca. 1992.*[13]

Version One:

(to be chanted)

Icky Dicky, I feel sicky,
Hasten, Jason, bring the basin.
Urp. Slop. Get the mop.

◆ *Mary, California, preteen ca. 1951-52.*

A cause of nausea, seasickness, is also a favorite subject, even among children who have never been on the open water:

Version Two:

(to be sung to the tune of "My Bonnie Lies Over the Ocean")

My body lies over the ocean,
My body lies over the rail.
I'm getting a sick new emotion,
Will someone bring me a pail?

Come up,
Come up,
Come up, sweet dinner. Come up. Come up.
(repeat)
Hasten, Jason.
Bring the basin.
Urp. Slop.
Bring the mop.

◆ *Suzanne, Oregon, age ten, 1993.*

Version Three:

(also to the tune of "My Bonnie Lies Over the Ocean")

My stomach is in a convulsion,
My head's hanging over the rail.
I don't want to dirty the ocean,
So someone please bring me a pail.
Come up, come up, come up my dinner,
Come up, come up,
Come up, come up, come up my dinner,
Come up.

(chanted)

Hasten, Jason,
Fetch the basin.
Oops, flop.
Get the mop.

This version was often followed by (to be said as a cheerleading chant):

Regurgitate! Regurgitate!
Throw up all the food you ate!
Vomit! Vomit!
Ye-a-a-h, VOMIT!

 Author Sherman, who heard it in several versions in New York City during the 1970s.[14]

❖

Still another common body function not usually discussed in polite adult conversation has to do with the nose, most specifically with mucus. Every child quickly becomes acquainted with nasal secretions, more so when he or she falls victim to a cold, and many a child is just as quickly warned by adults that picking one's nose is definitely not to be done, particularly not in public. This, of course, raises a challenge to child rhymesters, who are very happy to oblige:

(to the tune of "Everybody's Doing It")

Everybody's doing it,
Doing it, doing it,
Picking their nose
And chewing it, chewing it.
Tastes like candy, but it's not.

◆ *Hank, Boy Scout camp, Harlan, Kentucky, 1959 or 1960. The informant adds, "It's not" is run together to sound like "it's snot." Also known to author Sherman, ca. 1970s, Bronx, New York, in an incomplete version that consisted only of the first four lines.[15]*

ILLNESS

As children grow, they very quickly learn about the existence of disease, from the common cold to more life-threatening illnesses. A series of inoculations nowadays protects most children from such specters as polio and measles—but so strong is the terror of past generations that now curable diseases take their place along with more modern plagues in children's rhymes:

Version One:

(to be sung to the tune of "My Bonnie Lies Over the Ocean)

My mother had tuberculosis,
My father had only one lung.
They coughed up the blood by the buckets
And dried it for chewing gum.
Yum, yum,

Dried it for chewing gum.
Dentine, dentine,
Dried it for chewing gum.

◆ *Caryl, Rockford, Illinois, ca. 1940s.*

Version Two:

My Bonnie has tuberculosis,
My Bonnie has only one lung,
She coughs up great gobs of corruption
And rolls it around on her tongue.

◆ *Tom, Florida, late 1950s-early 1960s.*

Version Three:

My Grandma had tuberculosis,
It ate out one side of her lung,
She wokked (sic) up some bloody corruption,
And rolled it around on her tongue.

◆ *W.C., "the South," ca. 1970s.*

Version Four:

My Bonnie has tuberculosis,
My Bonnie has only one lung,
My Bonnie coughs up slimy green stuff
And dries it and chews it for gum.

Come up, come up,
Come up, dear dinner, come up, come up,
Come up, come up,
Come up, dear dinner, come up.

I'm coming, I'm coming,
Though my head is hanging low.
I hear those gentle voices calling

Section One: Getting Down to Basics

(Spoken)
Hasten, Jason, fetch the basin.
Oops, flop. Fetch the mop.

◆ *Adrienne, Anaconda, Montana, age twelve, 1960.*[16]

Another disease that once held a great deal of terror for most Americans—even though it has always been extremely rare in North America—was Hansen's Disease, popularly known as leprosy. Although it is now a curable disease, children's rhymes exaggerating its effects remain:

Version One:

(to be sung to the tune of "Jealousy")

Leprosy, it's crawling all over me,
There goes my ear, dear,
Into your beer, dear,
La, la, la, la, la, la,
Leprosy, it's crawling all over me,
There goes my eyeball, into your highball!

◆ *Diane, who learned it in elementary school in Los Angeles, California, ca. 1960. The informant was aware of other verses, but failed to recall them.*

Version Two:

Leprosy is crawling all over me.
There goes my foot, dear,
Into your root beer.
There goes my chin, dear,
Into your gin, dear.

◆ *Meg, who learned it at age ten in North Hollywood, California, ca. 1953-54. As with the previous informant, she knew there were more verses, but was unable to recall them.*[17]

However, not all illnesses recorded in children's rhymes are so deadly or permanently disfiguring:

(to be sung to the tune of "My Bonnie Lies Over the Ocean")

My body has calamine lotion.
My body's as sore as can be,
'Cause the flowers I picked for my grandma
Turned out to be poison ivy.

◆ *Katya, Fairborn, Ohio, ca. 1963.*[18]

DEATH AND DYING

Here is one of the biggest mysteries of human existence—and one of the most taboo of subjects for adults, at least in modern Western societies where death is considered something to be feared and ignored as much as possible. But, unlike adults, children refuse to let such a supremely important "Unknown" escape unscathed:

Version One:

Found a peanut, found a peanut, found a peanut on the floor,
Just now I found a peanut, found a peanut on the floor.
Cracked it open, cracked it open, cracked it open just now,
Just now I cracked it open, cracked it open just now.
It was rotten, it was rotten, it was rotten just now,
Just now it was rotten, it was rotten just now.
Ate it anyway, ate it anyway, ate it anyway just now,
Just now I ate it anyway, ate it anyway just now.
Got a stomachache, got a stomachache, got a stomachache
    just now,
Just now I got a stomachache, got a stomachache just now.

Operation, operation, operation just now,
Just now, operation, operation just now.
Went to heaven, went to heaven, went to heaven just now,
Just now I went to heaven, went to heaven just now.
I was dreaming, I was dreaming, I was dreaming just now,
Just now I was dreaming, I was dreaming just now.
Found a peanut, found a peanut, found a peanut on the
    floor,
Just now I found a peanut, found a peanut just now.

◆ *Kathryn, Girl Scout camp, age seven, 1994. A similar version was
contributed by Jeanne, North Carolina, ca. 1970.*

Version Two:

(follows same format as Version One)

Found a peanut, found a peanut, found a peanut just now,
Just now I found a peanut, found a peanut just now.
It was dirty ....
Ate it anyway ...
Got a tummyache ...
Saw the doctor ...
Died anyway ...
Went to heaven ...
Said a bad word ...
Went to the other place ...
Just now I went to the other place, went to the other place
    just now.

◆ *Hank, Benham, Kentucky, ca. 1950s.*

Version Three:

(follows same format as Version One)

Had a peanut, had a peanut, had a peanut just now,
Just now I had a peanut, had a peanut just now.

Broke it open ...
It was rotten ...
Ate it anyway ...
Got a bellyache ...
Saw the doctor ...
Had to operate ...
Died anyway ...
Went to heaven ...
Gate was locked ...
Went the other way ...
Didn't want me ...
Started over ...
Had a peanut,
Broke it open ...
It was rotten ...
Gave it away gave it away, gave it away just now,
Just now I gave it away, gave it away just now.

◆ *Informants, Katie, age fifteen, Megan, age fourteen, Tammy, age twelve, and Chelsey, age ten, sisters from Maysville, Washington, 1994.*[19]

The idea of suicide is repugnant to most adults but often all too intriguing to children and teenagers, most commonly the latter. Children, however, manage in their rhymes both to make fun of the adult feeling of horror and play upon the morbid lure of suicide—and, in the case of the following variations, to parody a commercial as well. In the late 1950s and early 1960s, Remco advertised a game called "Fascination" with a commercial sung to the French Canadian folk song "Alouette." While this, of course, helped the jingle stick in people's minds, it also made a parody almost inevitable:[20]

Version One:

Suffocation, Remco's Suffocation,
Suffocation, the game we love to play.
First you take a plastic bag,
Then you take a rubber bag,
Over the head, then you're dead,
Yayyyyy ....
(Repeat first two lines.)

◆ *Katie, northwest Chicago suburbs, 1955-1960. Dick knew this version in the Washington, D.C., suburbs, mid-1960s. A similar version was contributed by Martha, ca. 1971, Illinois.*

Version Two:

Suffocation, mental Retardation,
Suffocation, this is how you play:
First you take a plastic bag,
Then you put it on your head.
Go to bed, wake up dead.
Dea-ea-ea-ead.
(Repeat first two lines.)

◆ *Catherine, upper New Jersey, ca. 1969.*

Version Three:

Strangulation, strangu-strangulation,
Strangulation, the game we like to play.
First you take a big, brown rope,
Then you wrap it 'round your throat.
Go to bed.
Wake up dead.
Weeeeeeeeee ...
(Repeat first two lines.)

◆ *Abby, Pennsylvania, late 1960s-early 1970s.*

Version Four:

Suffocation, we like suffocation,
Suffocation, the game we like to play.

First you take a rubber hose,
Then you stick it up your nose,
Turn it on,
Then you drown.

Oh, oh, oh, oh.
(Repeat first two lines.)

◆ *J.F., Hawaii, ca. 1974. The informant adds, "(This is a) very old summer camp song. I don't remember all the verses, but there are about four of them."*[21]

But there are other rhymes about suicide that are quite unrelated to commercial parodies:

Won't you come with me to the kitchen,
To the kitchen, to the kitchen?
Won't you come with me to the kitchen,
And there, a date with death
We all shall keep!

We will turn on the gas in the oven,
In the oven, in the oven,
We will turn on the gas in the oven,
And there, a date with death
We all shall keep!

We will leave a note on the table,
On the table, on the table,
We will leave a note on the table,
"Milkman, don't leave us any milk to-daaay!"

◆ *Meg, Milwaukee, Wisconsin, ca. 1967.*

Sherman & Weisskopf

Almost worse to adult sensibilities than the thought of death is that of the body's subsequent dissolution. Children cheerfully tackle this unpleasant subject and ridicule the horror with deliberately disgusting exaggeration:

Version One:

Oh, do you know when the hearse rolls by,
That you may be the next to die?
They wrap you up in a dirty white sheet,
And throw you in a hole about six feet deep.

The worms crawl in, the worms crawl out,
The worms play pinochle on your snout.
Your chest caves in, your teeth fall out,
And the worms play pinochle on your snout!

The pus comes out like whipping cream,
The whole thing turns a sickly green—
You're dead, you're dead, you're dead!
And I forgot my spoon!

◆ *Lois, Lincoln Elementary School, South Bend, Indiana, 1950s. A similar version came from Katie, Northwest Chicago suburbs, ca. 1955-1960.*

Version Two:

…They nail you in and lower you down,
The men with shovels stand around.
They shovel in dirt and they throw in rocks,
And they don't give a damn if they break the box.

◆ *Jim, Bedford Village, New York, 1960s.*

Version Three:

Don't ever laugh when a hearse goes by,

Or you will be the next to die.
They'll cover you up with a big white sheet,
And bury you about six feet deep.
The worms crawl in, the worms crawl out,
They eat your guts and spit them out.
Your stomach turns a grassy green
And guts come out like shaving cream
For camel's eyes and moldy bread,
That's what you eat when you are dead.
Pray for the dead and the dead will pray for you.

◆ *Lisa, Chelsey, New York, ca. 1964.*

Version Four:

Never laugh when a hearse goes by,
Or you will be the next to die.
They wrap you in a bloody sheet,
And then they bury you six feet deep;
The worms crawl in, the worms crawl out,
The worms play pinochle on your snout;
Your eyes turn red, your skin turns green,
Your pus comes out like fresh whipped cream;
They eat your eyes, they eat your nose,
They eat the slime between your toes;
So never laugh when a hearse comes by,
Or you may be the next to die.
Pray for the dead and the dead will pray for you.
That is because they have nothing else to do.

◆ *Claire, Silver Spring, Maryland, 1960s.*

Version Five:

Did you ever think when the hearse goes by
That you may be the next to die?
They carry you off in a long black hack,
And don't ever think of coming back.

They wrap you up in a big white sheet
And bury you down about six feet deep.
They put you into a wooden box
And cover you up with dirt and rocks.
Everything is fine for about a week,
And then the coffin begins to leak.
Little green bugs with big green eyes
Crawl in your nostrils and out your fly.
The worms crawl in, the worms crawl out,
The worms play pinochle on your snout.
Then you turn a slimy green,
And pus comes out like whipping cream.
You sop it up with a piece of bread,
And that's what you eat when you are dead.

◆ Anna, *Springfield, Massachusetts, early 1960s.*

Version Six:

Did you ever think when a hearse goes by,
That you may be the next to die?
They wrap you up in a big white sheet,
And bury you down about six feet deep.
All goes well for about a week, and THEN—
The worms crawl in, the worms crawl out,
The worms play pinochle on your snout;
And little green men with little green eyes
Crawl into your nostrils and out of your fly;
Your stomach turns to a slimy green,
And pus comes out like whipping cream;
You sop it up with a piece of bread,
And that's what you eat when you are dead.

◆ JoAnn, *Louisiana, late 1960s.*

Version Seven:

A coffin came flying by,
And you're next to die.
Worms crawl in and worms crawl out
And turn your blood into sauerkraut.

◆ *Jessica, Montreal, Quebec, Canada, ca. 1960.*

Version Eight:

Oh when you see a hearse go by,
Do you ever think you'll be the next to die?
They grind your bones and drain your blood,
And bury you under six feet of mud.
The ants go in, the ants go out,
The ants play pinochle on your snout.
And then you turn an awful green,
Your guts come out like shaving cream,
And then you turn an awful red—
Do me a favor, please drop dead!

◆ *Cory, Toronto, Canada, 1980s.*[22]

But not everything that begins as an apparent gross-out
rhyme ends up as one. Sometimes, thanks to the primal, folkloric belief in magic that underlies even modern societies (the
most sophisticated of which retain such survivals as "knocking
on wood" or avoiding black cats), such a gross-out rhyme turns
into something else entirely:

Criss-cross applesauce.
Bugs crawling up your back, blood dripping down.
(repeated twice)
Bugs crawl up your back, they pinch you, they pinch you.
(repeated twice)
Bugs crawl down.

Wasps crawl up your back, they bite you, they bite you.
(repeated twice)
Wasps crawl down.
Now I'm going treasure-hunting,
But I'm mad because I can't find a treasure.
But look, there's the treasure!
Not here, not here, not here, not here.
But look at the spooky question-mark.
Now I'm going to get the mail, and there's a letter just for me.
I go into my house and there's a cake just for me.
I go into my room and open the window,
And there's a cool breeze,
And a slight squeeze,
And I see a bear that wants to pull your hair.

◆ *Katherine, Connecticut, age eleven, 1994. This is a ritual to get rid of headaches. According to the informant, there are movements that go with it, although we were given no further information about these. Neither the authors nor the informant have any clues as to the meaning of the various bits of symbolism involved in this ritual.*[23]

SECTION TWO:

DEALING WITH AUTHORITY

Just as a two year old gets into trouble by exploring the physical boundaries of the world with hands and feet, so too does an older child discover the social and cultural boundaries by exploring them with words. And it is not only boundaries of taboos centered on the body that the young explore with subversive verse. Defining the roles of others, especially those with power over them, and seeing how far one can go, is part of what the act of sharing subversive verse is about.[1]

In the first chapter of this section many of the verses cross the line between the passive/aggressive behavior of topping that occurs when children share gross-outs and the out-and-out insult. The rhymes are used in a ritualized way to define the group and to push the boundaries of what is acceptable. It is through these rhymes that the young discover what the "fighting words" are for their classmates. In the second chapter, youth is once again united, this time in the struggle against a common enemy, and the boundaries tested are those of the adults in positions of authority. The subject of children's ridicule in the final chapter is broader still. In this section, children tease not their intimates, nor specific authorities, but all of society.

CHAPTER FOUR:

PARENTS, FRIENDS, AND ENEMIES

PARENTS

While there are several children's folk rhymes about grandparents, there are relatively few rhymes about parents. This may possibly be because parents play such a vital part in children's lives that children are wary about insulting them—or perhaps, in a more primitive sense, risk endangering parents with rhymes involving them with injury or death.[1]

However, there are a few exceptions to every rule:

(to the tune of the commercial jingle, "I Love Bosco")

I hate Bosco,
It isn't good for me.
My mother put some in my milk
To try and poison me.
But I fooled mommy,
I put it in her tea,
And now I have no mommy

To try and poison me.

◆ *Bruce, Phoenix, New York, late 1950s. Similar versions come from Alan, Florida, ca. 1960s. who adds, "Powerful stuff, Bosco," and Rod, Linwood, California, age eight in early 1960s, and Claire, Maryland, mid-1960s.*[2]

FRIENDS AND ENEMIES

Just as there's a fine line between love and hate in adult relationships, so there is a fine line between the roles of friend and enemy in childhood—and children are not at all reluctant to cast the most enthusiastic insults about their fellows, whether those be close "pals," casual friends, outright foes, or even classroom outcasts. Children, as anyone with a decent memory can attest, are not at all sympathetic towards the weak or the different, and are definitely not shy about expressing their antipathy:

Version One:

Fatty and Skinny were laying in bed.
Fatty rolled over and Skinny was dead.
Fatty called the Doctor and the Doctor said:
"What's that pancake doing in the bed?"

◆ *Tom, Florida, ca. 1970s.*

Version Two:

Fatty and Skinny had a race.
Fatty fell down and broke his face.
Skinny thought it wasn't fair;
'Cause he lost his underwear!

◆ *Vera, Cambridge, Massachusetts, age four to eight, 1946-49.*[3]

While such Fatty and Skinny rhymes remain popular, children's insult rhymes are more likely to be in the form of personal than generalized attacks:

Version One:

Calvin (name) is a friend of mine,
He resembles Frankenstein.
When he does the Irish jig,
He looks more like Porky Pig!

◆ *Mary, northern Wisconsin, ca. 1955.*

Version Two:

(Name) is a friend of mine.
He resembles Frankenstein.
When he walks in through the door,
People faint and hit the floor.

◆ *Katya, Ohio, ca. 1963.*[4]

(to the themes of the "Tobar" cartoon
and the "Roto-Rooter" commercial jingle)

A prehistoric monster,
It came from outer space.
Its name is (kid's name)
And it has an ugly face.

The F.B.I. is helpless,
It's twenty stories tall.
What can we do?
Who can we call?

Call Roto Rooter,

That's the name.
And away go troubles
Down the drain.
Roto Rooter!

◆ *Sue, Brooklyn, New York, ca. 1967-75.*[5]

(Name of kid)'s a dope,
(S)he ate a bar of soap.
Bubbles here, bubbles there,
Bubbles in your underwear.

◆ *Sue, Brooklyn, New York, ca. 1967-75.*[6]

(Name) is a nut,
He has a rubber butt,
And every time he turns around,
It goes putt, putt.

◆ *Jeremy, Chicago, first grade ca. 1966.*[7]

❖

Some children's insult rhymes are region-specific. The following, referring to the Delaware River and Delaware Water Gap, is usually (though not exclusively) found among children who live or grew up along the East Coast:

Version One:

(to the tune of "The Old Grey Mare")

Here comes (name)
Walking down the Delaware,
Chewing up his/her underwear.
Couldn't find another pair.
Ten weeks later eaten by a polar bear.

And that was the end of him/her.

◆ *Sue, Brooklyn, New York, ca. 1967-1975. Similar versions were collected from Claire, Silver Spring, Maryland, ca. 1963-70, and Gregory, Bohemia, Long Island, age eleven in 1994.*[8]

Children also don't hesitate to attack their victims with melodies more commonly associated with holiday good will:

(to be sung to the tune of "Joy to the World")

Joy to the world, (name) is dead.
We barbequed his head.
What happened to the body?
We flushed it down the potty.
And round and round it goes,
And round and round it goes,
And round,
And round,
And round it goes.

◆ *Laura, Louisiana, age eight in 1994.*[9]

Children are very conscious of bad smells, particularly when they emanate—or are imagined to emanate—from other children:

I'm a monkey, you're a donkey;
I smell sweet and you smell funky.

◆ *Evelyn, reporting on her daughter Jacky and Jacky's friend Gina, Bronx, New York, 1970s. Informant tells us that this verse was the response of the black friend to being told she looked like a monkey. Both girls ended up crying, and have been close friends ever since.*

Some counting-out rhymes often have an edge of olfactory hostility to them:

Version One:

Inka bink,
A bottle of ink.
The cork fell off,
And you stink!

◆ *Claire, who learned it from her brother, Maryland, ca. 1960s. The informant adds, "It was one of the chants used to choose someone from the group (or eliminate all but one)."*

Version Two:

Inka, binka,
Bottle of ink.
The cork fell off,
And you stink!
Not because you're dirty,
Not because you're clean,
But because you kissed a boy behind a dirty magazine!

◆ *Judy, Michigan, late 1970s. This, too, is a counting-out rhyme.*

Version Three:

Candy apples on a stick make my tummy go 246,
Not because I'm dirty, not because I'm clean,
Just because I kissed a boy behind a magazine.
Hey, boys, how 'bout a fight?
Here comes Shannon on a mini-mini-bike.
She can wibble, she can wobble, she can do the splits,
But most of all, she can kiss, kiss, kiss.

◆ *Katie, Northwest Chicago suburbs, ca. 1955-1960. Similarly*

Christina, Arizona, 1990s. This version, unlike the previous two, is a jump-rope rhyme.

Version Four:

Down, down, baby, down by the roller coaster,
Sweet, sweet, baby, no place to go.
Caught you with your boyfriend, naughty, naughty,
Didn't do the dishes, lazy, lazy,
Stole a piece of candy, greedy, greedy,
Jumped out the window, must be crazy,
So.
Eeeny meeny pop-sa-leenie
Ou-a-pop-sa-leenie,
Education, liberation,
I love you—
NOT!

◆ *Informants, Reyla, age thirteen, 1994, and Meira, Rina and Eden, all age nine, 1994, Downsview, Ontario. Reyla and Meira are sisters, Rina and Eden are Meira's friends. The informants added that this was a hand-clapping chant.*

Version Five:

Saw ya with your boyfriend late last night ...
How do you know?
Peeked through the keyhole ...
Nosy!
Stole a piece of candy ...
Greedy!
Jumped out the window ...
Ya gotta be crazy!
Eenie, meenie, ichi-keenie,
Oh, ah, Halloweenie,
Hop-scotch Liberace,
Means-I-like-you-so: *(kiss).*

◆ *Karen, Syracuse, New York, 1980s. Informant notes a more popular last verse: "Means-I-hate-you-so, Phbthk!"*

Version Six:

Miss Mary Mack, Mack, Mack,
All dressed in black, black, black,
With silver buttons, buttons, buttons,
All down her back, back, back.
She cannot read, read, read,
She cannot write, write, write,
But she can smoke, smoke, smoke,
Her father's pipe, pipe, pipe.
She asked her mother, mother, mother
For fifteen cents, cents, cents
To see the boys, boys, boys,
Pull down their pants, pants, pants.
They pulled so low, low, low
They reached the snow, snow, snow.
They pulled so high, high, high,
They touched the sky, sky, sky.

◆ *Informants, Reyla, age thirteen, 1994, and Meira, Rina and Eden, all age nine, 1994, Downsview, Ontario. Reyla and Meira are sisters; Rina and Eden are Meira's friends. As with the previous version, the informants added that this was a hand-clapping chant.*[10]

Most children's insult rhymes are very explicitly worded, even if somewhat bizarre, but a few add some rather mysterious elements:

Version One:

Nanny nanny boo boo,
Stick your head in doo-doo!

Section Two: Dealing with Authority

◆ *"MoorHardi," Tallahassee, Florida, third grader, ca. 1970. The informant adds, "There was more to this, I think." Authors' note: The insult seems clear enough as it stands! Also known to Caroline, Huntsville, Alabama, late 1970s.*

Version Two:

Baby! Baby! Stick your head in gravy.
Wash it off with bubble gum
And send you to the Navy!

◆ *Sue, Brooklyn, New York, ca. 1967-75.*[11]

As noted before, children have very little patience with or sympathy for their fellows' weaknesses and will often "attack" another child with a biting rhyme at what seems to an adult like oddly mild provocation.

F___ a duck,
Screw a pigeon.
Go to hell
And learn religion.

◆ *Cliff, Elkton, Maryland, age eight, ca. 1952. The informant added that this was the response when anyone yelled "duck," and that it was also used "to get a kid's attention."*[12]

I was sitting sh___ing when I recieved your letter
The ground was bare and short of grass,
And with your letter
I wiped my ass.

◆ *Betty, Bronx, New York, early 1950s; known also to Jennifer, also Bronx, New York, late 1970s.*

One specialized form of insult rhyme is sometimes

referred to as "snaps," an almost ritualized form of verbal combat in which inner city children, usually boys of African-American descent, trade very blunt rhymes about each other, their families, or about that most sacred of subjects, their mothers, rather than blows:

Example One:

U-G-L-Y.
You ain't got no alibi.
You ugly!
You ugly!

Example Two:

M-O-M-M-A.
How do you think you got that way?
Your momma!
Your momma!

Example Three:

I seen your dog,
He's ugly too.
You must be twins.
He looks like you!

Example Four:

Two-four-six-eight,
We all know you masturbate.
You ugly!
You ugly!

◆ *Sue, who learned them from a camp-counselor friend, name not provided, who, in turn, learned them from inner-city children in Queens, New York, ca. 1992.*[13]

Children in more rural areas have their own forms of attack:

(fox whistle)
What a figure!
Two more legs,
You'd look like Trigger.

◆ *Elizabeth, eighth or ninth grade, 1958-59, Lamar Jr. High, McAllen, Texas. The informant notes that this is particularly effective because the initial whistle leads the victim to believe she is being noticed in an admiring way.*[14]

Hey hey, ho ho,
What's the matter with your afro, Negro?
Don't you know that sh__ don't grow?
Look at mine, ain't it fine?
I grease it all the time with Afro-Sheen and Vaseline.
That's how it stays so clean.

◆ *Caroline, Grissom High School, Huntsville, Alabama, ca. 1980s. Informant notes that this verse and the one following were used by the volleyball team to "pysch out" players on the opposing team with racial slurs, and were chanted in the same manner as less offensive cheers.*

Your mommy, your daddy,
Your greasy granny got a hole in her panty,
Go "wheet wheet wheet" down Sesame Street.
Go "toot toot toot" like a prostitute.

◆ *Caroline, Grissom High School, Huntsville, Alabama, ca. 1980s.*[15]

A variant on the insult rhyme is the one in which a child

is accused, not without a hint of implied admiration, of doing various daring but not quite illegal things:

Version One:

Policeman, policeman, do your duty,
Here comes (name), the American beauty.
She can wiggle, she can waggle, she can do the splits;
And she never wears dresses above her hips.
First comes love, then comes marriage,
Then comes (name) with a baby carriage.
How many children does she have?
One, two, three, four.
(This goes on until the girl jumping rope misses and is out.)

◆ Lee, *Academy of St. Aloysius, Jersey City, New Jersey, late 1950s-early 1960s.*[16]

Version Two:

Mailman, mailman,
Tutti Fruiti,
Here comes Missus
Macarooni.
She can do the pom-pom,
She can do the twist,
But most of all,
She can kiss, kiss, kiss.
K.I.S.S.

◆ *Meira, Downsview, Ontario, Canada, age nine, 1994. The informant adds, "I got this from kids while we were waiting at a dance recital. They didn't teach me, I got it just by watching." The informant's mother adds, "On the K.I.S.S. part, kids alternately angle out their heels and toes; eventually they get to where they're doing splits. The first one to fall over or give up is out."*[17]

The following verses also employ complicated motions combined with an insulting rhyme:

Mon chee-chee, mon chee-chee
I can play Atari *(Joystick pantomime).*
Mon chee-chee, mon chee-chee
Goin' on a safari *(march in place).*
Mon chee-chee, mon chee-chee
I know karate *(karate chop).*
Mon chee-chee, mon chee-chee
Oops, I'm not sorry *(after hitting person next to you).*

◆ *Karen, Syracuse, New York, 1980s.*

Another insult involving pantomime adds the idea of food adulteration:

("You hold your hand up in front of your chest as if you are praying, then you ask a friend to open the refrigerator. He/she parts your hands. Then you ask him/her to take out a Coke. He/she mimes taking out a Coke. You ask him/her to drink the Coke. He/she complies. Then you ask him/her to close the fridge. When he/she does, you sing the following ...")

(to the tune of "This Old Man")

Me Chinese—me play joke,
Me go peepee in your Coke!

◆ *Caroline, Grissom High School, Huntsville, Alabama, ca. mid-1980s.*[18]

Team spirit may be something drilled into children by adults, but the tribal instinct is built into us all. Everyone can

name an "us against them" situation, whether it be race, nation-
ality, gender, sexual orientation, or simply different ways of
doing things that provides the dividing line:[19]

Version One:

(to the tune of "We Will, We Will Rock You")

We will, we will, you know what,
Kick your butt
All the way to Pizza Hut.
While you're there, comb your hair,
Then we'll take your underwear.

◆ *Michelle, Bronx, New York, age six in 1994. The informant adds
that both girls and boys sing this song.*

Version Two:

We will, we will,
We'll kick your butt to Pizza Hut.
Comb your hair, comb your hair,
And don't forget your underwear.
Is it black? Is it blue?
Oh my gosh, it's full of poo!

◆ *Laura, Louisiana, age eight in 1994.*[20]

This "tribal" combat can be on a more personal level,
though it definitely bears a relationship to the two previous
rhymes:

(to the tune of "Ta-Ra-Ra-Boom-Der-Ay")

Ta-ra-ra-boom-der-ay,
I took your pants away,
And while you're standing there,

I took your underwear.

◆ *"MoorHardi," Tallahassee, Florida, third grader, ca. 1970.*[21]

The "us against them" sense often carries through into games in which what is on the surface a friendly group of children harbors oddly hostile undertones:

(Name) is it!
(Name) is it!
He's a stupid idiot!

◆ *Lorelei, Glen Ellyn, Illinois, age eight, 1994. The informant's mother, Lindalee, adds, "(This) variant of tag my daughter plays (which is called 'Flush') is they try and push down the arm of the person who is it like they are flushing the toilet."*[22]

There's a certain tribal feeling about a one's own classmates or, on a slightly larger scale, a child's own grade at school that leads to a form of fighting chant:

First grade babies,
Second grade cats,
Third grade angels,
Fourth grade rats.

◆ *Myekia, fifth grade, Park Hill Public School, North Little Rock, age nine in 1994.*[23]

Some fight songs manage to slip in an unexpected twist as well, almost but not quite turning "dirty":

Rah, rah, ree,
Kick 'em in the knee.

Rah, rah, rass.
Kick 'em in the other knee!

◆ *Deborah, Germany, ca. 1960s. Also known to author Weisskopf, Huntsville, Alabama, 1978-79, who learned it from Marsha, a fellow marching-band member.*[24]

There are also, not surprisingly, some songs that pit boys against girls, pretending (depending on which gender is doing the singing) to show the superiority of one over the other:

Version One:

S.O.-S.O.-S.O.S.
My mother your mother lives across the street,
1819 Blueberry Street.
Every night they had a fight,
And this is what they said tonight.
Boys go to Venus—cut off their penis.
Girls go to Mars to be superstars.
Boys are rotten—made of cotton.
Girls are dandy—made of candy.
Boys go to Jupiter—get more stupider.
Girls go to college—get more knowledge.

◆ *Joanna, Montreal, Quebec, Canada, age eight in 1994. The informant's fourteen-year-old sister also added a variant line: "Girls go to Mars to eat chocolate bars and meet superstars." Although not so specified by the informant, this is probably intended as a jump-rope rhyme.*

Version Two:

Boys got the muscles,
Teachers got the brains,
Girls got the sexy legs,
And we won the games.

◆ *Colleen, age eleven, and Liana, age seventeen, 1994, Hastings and Yonkers, New York, respectively. Colleen added that this rhyme was usually chanted by girls at boys, and sometimes, just for the sake of nonsense, had the lines scrambled so they came out, "Teachers got the muscles," etc.*[25]

But not all rhymes are girls against boys or one group of children against another or against an unfortunate individual. Some are pure defiance against the adult world:

Version One:

(to the tune of "Yankee Doodle Dandy")

Oh, we are juvenile delinquents,
Marijuana do or die.
We drink with soldiers and we neck with bums,
We wait on the corner 'till our pick-up comes.

Oh, we are juvenile delinquents,
We never, ever sleep alone.
Move over Charlie, you're hogging up the whole damn bed,
And there goes Granny
Swingin' on the outhouse door
Without a nightie,
And Grandpa couldn't ask for more
'Cause she was nude,
'Cause she was nude.

◆ *Sue, Brooklyn, New York, ca. 1970s.*

Version Two:

Oh, I'm a juvenile delinquent,
Afraid to go home any more.
I drink with the sailors and I smoke with the bums,
Waiting on the corner till my pickup comes.

Oh, I'm a juvenile delinquent,
Afraid to go home any more.
My Daddy beats me
(Afraid to go home any more),
My momma hates me
(Afraid to go home any more),
And then there's Gramma
Swingin' on the outhouse door,
Without her nightie,
Swingin' on the outhouse door,
And then there's Grampa,
Moppin' up the outhouse floor,
With Gramma's nightie,
Moppin' up the outhouse floor.

◆ *Elizabeth, Camp Reily, Harrisburg, Pennsylvania, ca. 1977.*[26]

In this vein of defiance, some children take a stereotypical insult image and turn it into a tongue-in-cheek war chant:

Clap your hands! *(stomp feet)*
Stamp your feet! *(clap hands)*
Dumb blonds can't be beat! *(beat breast with right fist)*
What are we? Dumb!
What are we? Dumb!
What are we? Dumb!
We're number one, *(hold up peace sign)*
So peace! *(hold up one finger)*

◆ *Reyla, Downsview, Ontario, Canada, age thirteen, 1994.*[27]

Some insult rhymes center on that most important personal date to a child, his or her birthday:

Version One:

(to the tune of "Happy Birthday to You")

Happy Birthday to you,
You live in a zoo.
You look like a monkey,
And you act like one, too!

◆ *Elissa, Syracuse, New York, 1960s. Also known to Annie, Brooklyn, New York, ca. 1971-72; Jim, Connecticut, 1960s, who knew a variant with the last line, "And you smell like one too"; author Sherman, Bronx, New York, 1960s; author Weisskopf, Brooklyn, New York, 1960s; Sue, Brooklyn, New York, ca. 1967-75; and Claire, Silver Spring, Maryland, ca. 1963-1970.*

Version Two:

(to be sung to the tune of "The Volga Boatman")

Happy Birthday (ugh),
Happy Birthday (ugh).
There is sorrow in the air,
People dying everywhere,
But happy birthday (ugh).

◆ *Tina, Bronx, New York, ca. 1960s.*

Version Three:

Happy Birthday.
Happy Birthday.
Worms and germs are in the air,
People dying everywhere.
Happy Birthday.

◆ *Susan, Ohio, ca. 1960s.*[28]

But not all of the rhymes recited by children are hostile to others. Some seem so downright banal and cute that one has to wonder if these friendship songs were actually originally designed by adults for children, even if the songs are in the domain of folklore by now:

Version One:

Ceecee, my playmate,
Come out and play with me.
And bring your dollies three,
Climb up my apple tree.
Slide down my rainbow
Into my cellar door.
And we'll be jolly friends
Forever more, more,
Shut the door.

◆ *Informants, Reyla, age thirteen, and Meira, age nine, 1994, Downsview, Ontario, Canada. The informants added that this was a hand-clapping rhyme.*

However, the folk process being what it is, and children (over the age of five or so) having the small tolerance they have for cuteness, we were also able to collect the following, definitely not cutesy, version:

Version Two:

Say, say, my vampire,
Come out and bite me.
And bring your bats three,
Climb up my graveyard tree,
And slide down my tombstone
Into my coffin door.
And we'll be blood-sucking vampires

Forever more, more,
(*pause*)
More, more, more.

◆ *Jerri, Doraville, Georgia, ca. 1971-72.*[29]

Some rhymes make fun not of other children but of truisms. All children—and a good many adults—delight in nonsense, and there are a good many children's rhymes that seem at first to be the beginning lines of a familiar adage but turn out, thanks to unexpected twists, to be total non sequiturs:

Thirty days hath September,
April, June and no wonder.
All the rest eat peanut butter,
Save Grandmother—and she drives a Buick.

◆ *Daniel, Eagle, Alaska, ca. 1974-1980. The informant learned this from his father, who came from California. Jeanne knew a version that ended with, "Except my grandmother, who drives a little red wagon," North Carolina, ca. 1970.*[30]

Another common form of nonsense rhyme that children enjoy reciting seems at first to be one that tells a story in the form of an "official" proclamation but actually turns out to be nothing but doubletalk:

Version One:

Ladies and gentlemen, hoboes and tramps,
Cockeyed mosquitoes and bowlegged ants,
The admission is free—just pay at the door,
Pull out a chair and sit on the floor.

Late in the morning, and early in the night,

Two dead boys got up to fight.
They stood back-to-back, and faced each other,
Turned around and shot each other.

◆ *Deborah, on a U.S. military base in Germany, mid-1960s.*

Version Two:

In the bright, bright day,
In the middle of the night,
Two dead boys got up to fight.
They went back to back,
Faced each other,
Drew out their swords
And shot each other.
A deaf policeman heard the noise,
Went out to kill the two dead boys.
Now if you don't believe that my lie is true,
Ask the blind man—
He saw it, too!

◆ *Colin, Montreal, Quebec, Canada, age twelve, 1994. Similarly, Debbie, probably learned in junior high school, Syracuse, New York, ca. 1970s, and Sue, Brooklyn, New York, ca. 1967-75.*

Version Three:

Ladies and jelly spoons,
Hoboes and tramps,
Cross-eyed mosquitoes
And bow-legged ants,
I come before you
To stand behind you
To tell you of something
I know nothing about.
This Thursday, which will be Good Friday,
There will be a meeting at the four corners

Of the Round Table.
The subject will be Christopher Clumsy's
Journey up the Mississisloppy.

◆ *Fran, Jackson, Mississippi, young teen, ca. 1970s. The informant learned this from Susan, age sixteen, and Karen, an adult, all from Jackson.*

Version Four:

Ladies and gentlemen, uncles and aunts,
Cockeyed mosquitoes and bow-legged ants.
I come here before you to stand behind you
And tell you something I know nothing about.
Next Wednesday, which is Good Friday,
There's a ladies' meeting for men only.
No admission, pay at the door,
Pull up a chair and sit on the floor.

◆ *Daniel, Eagle, Alaska, 1976 or 1977. The informant learned this from "the Ostrander boys" who had moved to Eagle from Michigan.*[31]

CHAPTER FIVE:

ORGANIZED DEFIANCE: SCHOOL, CHURCH, AND CAMP

SCHOOL

Once children leave infancy, one of the major influences on their lives becomes school. While children may secretly enjoy learning, they also, quite understandably, can harbor a great deal of resentment over having their days structured and their freedom curtailed. They generally relieve this resentment not by engaging in actual violence but by reciting rhymes featuring caricatured, almost ritualized violence. Versions one through five share essentially the same first five lines:

Version One:

(to be sung to the tune of "The Battle Hymn of the Republic")

Mine eyes have seen the glory of the burning of the school.
We have tortured every teacher, we have broken every rule.
We have thrown away our homework and we hanged the
    principal.
Our school is burning down.

◆ *Jim, St. Patrick's Parochial School, Bedford, New York, ca. 1960s.*

Sherman & Weisskopf

Version Two:

… We have broken all the blackboards so
The teachers can not write.
And the kids keep marching on!

◆ *Susan, Stadium Drive Grade School, Boardman, Ohio, late 1950s.*

Version Three:

… The principal is dead
'Cause we shot him in the head
And that's why there's no more school.

◆ *Author Weisskopf, Brooklyn, New York, mid-1970s.*

Version Four:

… We have sat in every corner of this dirty rotten school.
Our truth is marching on.

Glory, glory hallelujah,
Teacher hit me with a ruler.
I met her at the door
With a loaded .44,
And she ain't my teacher no more.

Glory, glory hallelujah,
Teacher hit me with a ruler.
I met her at the bank
With a loaded Army tank,
And she ain't my teacher no more.

Glory, glory hallelujah
Teacher hit me with a ruler.
I caught her on the run
With a really big shot gun,
And she ain't my teacher no more.

◆ *Kari, Minnesota, mid-1970s.*

Version Five:

... We have crucified the principal and
Kicked him out the door,
And the teacher ain't teachin' no more!

Glory, glory hallelujah
Teacher hit me with a ruler.
The ruler turned red and the teacher dropped dead,
And the teacher ain't teachin' no more!

♦ *Lynn, Willingboro, New Jersey, ca. mid-1960s.*

Version Six:

... We have tortured every teacher,
And we broke the golden rule.
We have torn up all the math books,
And the principal's a fool,
As we go marching on!

Glory, glory, how peculiar!
Glory, glory, how peculiar!
Glory, glory, how peculiar!
As we go marching on!

♦ *Sue, Brooklyn, New York, ca. 1967-75.*

Version Seven:

Today's the day we celebrate the burning of the school.
We've tortured every teacher and we've broken every rule.
We went and hanged the principal and shot the PTA,
And the kids are running on.

♦ *Brendan, Colebrook, New Hampshire, age nine, 1994.*[1]

Many informants knew parodies of the chorus only.

Version One:

Glory, glory, hallelujah,
Teacher coming with a ruler.
I bopped her on the bean with a rotten tangerine,
And she won't be coming 'round no more.

♦ *Author Sherman, Bronx, New York, 1960s. Also contributed by Susan, Boardman, Ohio, late 1950s; Alan, Boston area, Massachusetts, 1950s; Cindy, Denver, Colorado, ca. 1964; Claire, Silver Spring, Maryland, 1960s; Ellie, Queens, New York, ca. 1969; and Valerie, Modina, New York, 1960s. Susan's variation: "I hit her on the bean with a rotten tangerine/And boy, did she turn green!" Alan: "I bopped her on the bean with a rotten tangerine/And now her teeth are green." Claire: "I bopped her on the beam with a rotten tangerine/And the juice came dripping down." Ellie: "I hit his baldy bean/With a rotten tangerine." Valerie's version contained the rotten tangerine and the line, "And her teeth came marching out."*

Version Two:

... I hit him on the spot
With a rotten apricot,
And his teeth went marching on.

♦ *Hank, Benham, Kentucky, ca. 1957-1960.*

Version Three:

... I slapped her in the eye
With a piece of apple pie.
(last line missing.)

♦ *Beth, New Jersey, ca. 1970.*

Version Four:

... I shot her in the seater
With a .22 repeater,

And she (he) ain't comin' back no more!

◆ *Deborah, Honolulu, Hawaii, ca. 1980s. The informant adds, "Instead of 'teacher,' one can also insert [an] appropriate name, i.e. Mrs. Miller, etc."*

Version Five:

... I met her at the door with a loaded .44,
And she ain't gonna teach no more.

◆ *Jim, St. Patrick's Parochial School, Bedford, New York, ca. 1960s. Similar versions were contributed by Susan, Boardman, Ohio, ca. late 1950s; Robin, New Bedford, Massachusetts, ca. 1973; David, central Virginia, late 1960s; and Katherine, Connecticut, age ten, 1994. A similar version with a last line, "And she ain't my teacher no more," is known to Robert, New York, ca. late 1950s. Jim also knew a milder third line—"I hit her on the butt with a rotten coconut"—as did Claire, Maryland, ca. 1960s—as well as the complete second version which follows:*

Version Six:

... Bopped her on the bean with a rotten tangerine,
And she sank to the floor like a German submarine.[2]

Version Seven:

... I met her at the door with an ought-ought forty-four,
And there ain't no teacher anymore!

◆ *Elissa, Syracuse, New York, ca. 1960s.*

Version Eight:

... I shot her through the attic
With a German automatic,
And she don't teach no more.

◆ *Cindy, Denver, Colorado, ca. 1964.*

Version Nine:

... I met her in the attic
With a loaded automatic,
And she ain't our teacher no more, no more,
And she ain't our teacher no more.

◆ *Brendan, Colebrook, New Hampshire, age nine, 1994.*

Version Ten:

... I met her at the bank
With a loaded Sherman tank.
And my teacher ain't teachin' no more.

◆ *Jim, Connecticut, ca. 1970s. Also known to Brendan, Colebrook, New Hampshire, age nine, 1994, with the variant line, "With a U.S. Army tank."*

Version Eleven:

... Ruler turned red
And the teacher lost her head,
And that's why there's no more school.

◆ *Author Weisskopf, Brooklyn, New York, 1970s.[3]*

Every now and then in children's folk rhymes, the teacher does win:

Version Twelve:

... Kicked me out of class
And I landed on my ass ...
(last line missing.)

◆ *Dave, Waterloo, Wisconsin, 1970s.[4]*

❖

But "The Battle Hymn of the Republic" is far from being the only tune used for anti-teacher and anti-school children's parodies:

Version One:

(to be sung to the tune of "Ta-Ra-Ra-Boom-Der-Ay")

Ta-ra-ra-boom-de-yay,
My teacher passed away.
I shot her yesterday
And threw her in the bay.
And when they took her out,
She smelled like sauerkraut.

◆ *Martha who learned this in the late 1960s from an unnamed friend from Seattle. The informant adds about this song, "Repeat ad nauseum."*

Version Two:

Ta-ra-ra-boom-de-yay
There is no school today!
Our teacher passed away,
We killed her yesterday!
As for the principal,
He's in the hospital!
As for the secretary,
She's in the cemetery!

◆ *Cory, Toronto, Canada, 1970s.*

❖

Other well-known tunes also come in for their share of children's anti-school parodies:

Version One:

(to be sung to the tune of "On Top of Old Smokey")

On top of the schoolhouse,
All covered with blood,
I shot my poor teacher
With a forty-four slug.
I went to her funeral,
I went to her grave.
Some people threw flowers,
I threw a grenade.
I opened her coffin,
She wasn't quite dead,
So I took a bazooka
And blew off her head.

◆ *Katzi, Colebrook Elementary School, Colebrook, New Hampshire, age nine, 1994. An almost identical version was contributed by Katherine, Connecticut, age ten, 1994. Similar versions came from Claire, who learned it from a friend, who learned it in St. Louis, Missouri, in the 1970s. Also known to Mitch, Suffolk, Long Island, New York, 1972.*

Version Two:

On top of Old Smoky
All covered with sand
I shot my poor teacher
With a red rubber band.
I shot her with glory,
I shot her with pride.
How could I have missed her,
She's forty-feet wide.

◆ *David, age seven, who learned this from his cousin, Jennifer, age ten, both from Celo, North Carolina, 1994. Also Karen, Syracuse, New York, 1980s.*

Version Three:

On top of Old Smoky
All covered with sand
I shot my poor teacher
With a green rubber band.

(line missing)
I shot her with pride.
I couldn't miss her,
She was fifty-feet wide.

I went to her funeral,
I went to her grave.
Some people threw flowers,
I threw a grenade.

I opened her coffin,
She still wasn't dead.
I took a bazooka
And blew off her head.

◆ *Gregory, Bohemia, Long Island, age eleven, 1994. The informant
learned this on the school bus from his older brother, and provided
the following partial version as well:*

Version Four:

On top of the school house
All covered with blood
I shot my poor teacher
With a fifty-foot gun.

Version Five:

On top of Old Smokey
Where nobody goes
I saw (female teacher)
Without any clothes.

Along came (male teacher)
And took off his vest,
And when he saw (female teacher),
He took off the rest.

◆ *"M.J.," Hammond, Indiana, early 1960s.*[5]

Nor are the melodies of Christmas carols spared:

Version One:

(to be sung to "Joy to the World")

Joy to the world, the school burned down,
And all the teachers died.
We're going to take the principal
And hang her from the toilet bowl
With a rope around her neck,
A rope around her neck,
A rope, a rope around her neck.

◆ *Katzi, Colebrook Elementary School, Colebrook, New Hampshire, age nine, 1994.*

Version Two:

Joy to the world, my teacher's dead,
I chopped right off his head.
Don't worry 'bout the body
I flushed it down the potty,
I watched it go around,
I watched it go 'round and 'round.

◆ *Gregory, Bohemia, Long Island, age eleven, 1994. Also known to David, age seven, who learned it from his cousin, Jennifer, age ten, 1994, Celo, North Carolina.*

Version Three:

Joy to the world, the teacher's dead,
We barbecued her head.
What happened to her body?
We flushed it down the potty.
And around and around it went,
And around and around it went,
And around and around and around it went.

Joy to the world, the school burned down,
And all the teachers are dead.
If you're looking for the principal,
He's hanging from the flagpole
With a rope around his neck,
With a rope around his neck,
With a rope, a rope around his neck.

♦ *Informants, Becky, age eleven, and Mark, age nine, North Carolina, 1994. They are, incidentally, not acquainted with David or Jennifer, also from North Carolina, as noted in Version Two.* [6]

Version One:

Deck the halls with boughs of holly.
Fa la la la la la la la la.
'Tis the season to be naughty.
Fa la la la la la la la la.
Break a window, start a fire,
Fa la la la la la la la la.
Put a nail in teacher's tire.
Fa la la la la la la la la.

♦ *Jessie, Jewett Street School, Manchester, New Hampshire, age eight to ten, ca. 1988.*

Version Two:

Deck the halls with gasoline
Fa la la la la la la
Light a match and watch it gleam
Fa la la la la la la
Watch the school burn down to ashes
Fa la la la la la la
Aren't you glad you played with matches?
Fa la la la la la la.

♦ *Gregory, Bohemia, Long Island, age eleven, 1994. The informant learned this on the school bus, fittingly enough on the last day before Christmas vacation.*[7]

Some children's anti-school rhymes have no melody at all, but are meant to be chanted:

Eeny meeny miney moe,
Catch your teacher by the toe.
If he squirms, squeeze it tight
Then you take a great big bite
(Chomp noise.)

♦ *Gregory, Bohemia, Long Island, age eleven, 1994.*[8]

But children are not content to merely use Christmas carols or inspirational melodies for their parodies:

Version One:

(to the tune of "Row, Row, Row Your Boat")

Row, row, row your boat
Gently down the stream.
Throw the teacher overboard,

Listen to her scream.

◆ *Linnea, Pennsylvania, ca. 1963. Also contributed by Cindy, Denver, Colorado, ca. 1964, and Jim, Westchester, New York, ca. 1960s.*

Version Two:

Row, row, row your boat
Gently down the stream.
Throw the teacher overboard
And listen to her scream.

Five days later
Send her down the Delaware,
Eating dirty underwear.
Couldn't find another pair.

Five days later
Find her kissing a polar bear.
That's how
The polar bear died.

◆ *K.S., second grade, West Campus Central School, Tulsa, Oklahoma, 1985.*[9]

(to the tune of the "Chiquita Banana" commercial jingle)

I'm a chiquita banana and I'm here to say,
Get rid of your teacher the easy way.
Put a banana peel on the floor
And watch your teacher fly out the door.

If another teacher comes into class,
Put another banana on the floor
And she'll break her ...

◆ *Janni Lee, Long Island, New York, ca. 1980.*[10]

(to the tune of "Whistle While You Work")

Hi ho, hi ho,
It's off to school we go,
With hand grenades and razor blades,
Hi ho, hi ho, hi ho.

♦ *Author Weisskopf who learned it from Marsha, Huntsville, Alabama, 1979.*[11]

Version One:

(to the tune of the "Marine's Hymn")

(first lines missing)
We will fight for lunch and recess
And to keep our desks a mess.
We are proud to claim the title
Of the teacher's little pests.

♦ *Claire, Silver Spring, Maryland, ca. 1960s.*

Version Two:

From the halls of Flower Valley
To the (something) of PTA,
We will fight our teachers daily
With spitballs, mud, and clay.
We will fight for lunch and recess,
And will keep our desks a mess.
From the halls of Flower Valley
To the teacher's number one pests!

♦ *"Electro," New Jersey, late 1970s. The informant adds, "Flower Valley was my elementary school; other names could be plugged in."*[12]

But not all child-teacher parodies end in violence. The following could just as well have been sung by a teacher!

(to the tune of "Hark the Herald Angels Sing")

Hark the Herald Angels shout,
___ more days till we get out.
Grab your ball, grab your chain,
And run like Hell for the nearest train.

◆ *Phronsie, Miami, Florida, late 1950s or early 1960s.*[13]

Once children begin to leave childhood and elementary school behind, their songs begin to feature different themes. Alcohol and drunkenness are favorite subjects of high school and college songs, even among students who really aren't part of drunken outings:

(to the tune of "The Caissons Go Rolling Along")

Give a cheer, give a cheer,
For the nuns who make the beer,
In the basement of St. Patrick's School.

◆ *Jim, St. Patrick's Parochial School, Bedford, New York, 1960s.*[14]

The following is a widely known parody, used either to boast about the drinking abilities of a particular school's students, or to make a general jesting boast:

Version One:

(to the tune of the Notre Dame fight song)

Beer, beer for Old Bozeman High,

Bring on the whiskey, bring on the rye.
Send some freshmen down for gin,
And don't let a sober person in (Rah! Rah! Rah!)

We never stagger, we never fall,
We sober up on wood alcohol,
As our loyal boys come marching
Back to the bar for
Back to the bar for
Back to the bar for more.

♦ *Informants, Fern, age fifteen in the 1940s, and Adrienne, who learned the same version as a young teen in the 1970s, both from Bozeman, Montana. Informant Adrienne adds that the name of any school could be inserted.*

Version Two:

Cheer, cheer for old Whiskey High!
You bring the whiskey, I'll bring the rye.
Send the freshmen out for gin,
And don't let a sober sophomore in.
We never stumble, we never fall,
We sober up on wood alcohol,
While the profs and deans are lying
Drunk on the barroom floor.

♦ *Author Sherman, New York City, probably late 1970s. Sometimes the song ended with a rousing "Rah! Rah! Rah!" Sometimes the school name was changed to "Old Rotgut High." A similar version, with the first line "… Sandy Springs High," was collected from Debbie, who learned it from a friend who attended Sandy Springs High School in Georgia in the 1970s.*

Version Three:

Beer, beer for old Huntsville High,
You bring the whiskey,

I'll bring the rye.
Send the freshmen out for gin,
And don't let a sober sophomore in.
We never stagger, we never fall,
We sober up on wood alcohol.
All the loyal faculty are drunk on the bandroom floor.

◆ *Author Weisskopf, ninth grade, Huntsville High School, Huntsville, Alabama, early 1980s. This version was specific to the marching band, who had a need to fight the stereotype of being uncool "band fags." These are also the only words to the school fight song she knows.*[15]

Drugs emerge in their share of high school and college songs as well, even among those students who have no intention of trying to get high:

Version One:

(to the tune of "Frere Jacque")

Marijuana, Marijuana,
LSD, LSD.
The principal (insert name) makes it
And the teachers take it.
Why can't we?

◆ *Brick, Silver Spring, Maryland, late 1960s-early 1970s.*

Version Two:

Marijuana, marijuana,
LSD, LSD.
Rockefeller makes it,
Mayor Lindsay takes it.
Why can't we? Why can't we?

◆ *Sue, Brooklyn, New York, late 1960s-early 1970s.*[16]

One of the delights of the student is that of mocking one's school song or of making fun of the school itself, turning it—at least in parody—into a prison or slum or even toxic waste site:

Version One:

(to be sung to "The Whiffenpoof Song")

Near the manor of Van Cortlandt,
Near the old Van Cortlandt Still,
Stands a school we're not so proud of
High on Indigestion Hill.
It's a school where none are busy,
A place where kids don't thrive.
It's a school where none are happy.
Oh P.S. 95.

For we are marching on together
Beneath the hammer and the sickle;
We are working in all weather
Though a\our teacher looks like a pickle.

And for the welfare of our country,
And for our neighbors we don't thrive,
As we learn to burn Old Glory
Here in 95.

◆ *Tina, elementary school student, ca. 1960, Bronx, New York. The informant adds, "Apologies to Hank Mudge. We were very young." Informant gives us two versions of verse two, indicated by the slash mark in the last line.*

Version Two:

On the shores of West Poe Ditch,
So deep and thick and wide,
Stands an old deserted outhouse

Known as Bowling Green Senior High.

◆ *John, Detroit area, late 1960s. The informant adds, "I cannot remember the straight words to that. West Poe Ditch, by the way, at the time had the distinction of being on the EPA's list as the longest remaining unclosed sanitary sewer in the USA. Just one more thing that makes the little town I came from special."*

Version Three:

On the banks of old Kanawha,
Pointing to the sky,
Stands an old abandoned outhouse:
Stonewall Jackson High.

◆ *Dan, West Virginia, ca. 1970s.*

Version Four:

O Mount Holyoke, we pay thee tuition,
In the fervor of youth that's gone wrong;
Each year it gets higher and higher,
My God, Alma Mater, how long?

So from barroom to bedroom we stagger,
And united in free love for all,
Our drinks are too strong and our morals gone,
Mount Holyoke, what's happ'ning to meeeeee?
Mount Holyoke, what's happ'ning to me?

◆ *Judy, Mount Hadley, Mass., ca. 1970s. The informant, pointing to the subversive power of a good parody, adds, "That is so pervasive that when we fired up the Alma Mater at my graduation, no one remembered the straight version. The president started, looked around, grinned, and swung into the parody along with the rest of us. So we went out as we had come in: sideways."*[17]

School rivalries, that is, the proclaimed superiority of one's own school over another, are also sources of childhood rhymes. Both the rivalries and the idea of such rhymes tend to last right through college days, though they understandably get more explicit in their insults as children grow up:

Version One:

(to be sung to "High Above Cayuga's Waters")

High above Cayuga's waters
There's an awful smell.
Does it come from Lake Cayuga,
Or is it Cornell?

◆ *Susan, Youngstown, Ohio, 1970s. A similar version was collected from Tina, Bronx, New York, 1970s.*

Version Two:

High above Cayuga's waters,
Comes an awful smell,
Seven thousand sons of bitches
Call themselves Cornell.

◆ *John, Baton Rouge, Louisiana, 1970s.*

Version Three:

High above Cayuga's waters,
There's an awful smell,
Some say it's Cayuga's waters,
Some say it's Cornell.
Air polluting, jock recruiting,
We're saluting you.
(Obscene gesture—the arm, not the finger)

◆ *Claire, Silver Spring, Maryland, who recently learned it from a*

Brown alum who told her that "he couldn't write it down because it was strictly an oral tradition. Well, I'm not from Brown."[18]

But sometimes the parody isn't aimed at any specific school or school rivalry:

Version One:

(chanted)

Rooty toot toot,
Rooty toot toot,
We are the boys from the institute.
We don't drink or smoke or chew
And we don't go out with girls that do.
Nyah nyah ny-nyah nyah nyah.
Our class won the Bible!

◆ *P.R., Montana and Wisconsin, ca. 1958.*

Version Two:

Rooty toot toot,
Rooty toot toot,
We are the girls from the institute.
We don't smoke and we don't chew
And we don't go with boys who do.
Our class won the Bible!

◆ *Author Sherman, Bronx, New York, 1960s.*[19]

CAMP AND SCOUTING ACTIVITIES

While most parodies of "official" songs center around schools, there are other adult-created songs about such institutions as Scouting that children sometimes parody as well, particularly when the original words, praising a troop's merits, become just a bit too nice for children to bear:

> Oh, we're the Scouts of Region Four you hear so much
> about.
> The ladies hide their pocketbooks whenever we go out.
> We barely can remember all the rotten things we do.
> We like to lie and cheat and steal, especially to you.

◆ *John, 1970s. The informant adds that Region 4 comprised Ohio, Kentucky and West Virginia.*[20]

This is a parody of a camp song, similar to the many parodies of school songs:

> *(to the tune of "Alma Mater")*
>
> Weetamo, the camp of stinkers,
> By a lake of ink,
> Guided by a bunch of counselors,
> Weetamo, you stink.

◆ *Vera, Girl Scout camp, Massachusetts, early 1950s.*[21]

Unlike parodies of scouting, most parodies about life at camp center not around the accomplishing of good deeds—or the boasting over doing bad ones—but around adult restrictions:

Version One:

> I go to Camp (name), so pity me.
> There's not a boy in the vicinity.
> And every night at nine they lock the door.

I don't know why the hell I ever came before.
I'm gonna pack my bags and homeward bound.
I'm gonna turn this damn camp upside down.
I'm gonna smoke and drink and neck and
pet and what the heck.
The hell with this whole damn camp.
(tune change)
And (camp director) swinging by the outhouse door—
Without his undies.
What the hell are undies for?
To catch pneumonia.

◆ *Tina, New York State, late 1960s. A similar version is known to author Sherman, Pennsylvania at Girl Scout camp, 1970s; the author also has heard it sung, with only the slightest alterations, at New York City's all-girl Walton High School.*

Version Two:

I come from Valley View, so pity me.
There's not a boy in the vicinity.
And every night at nine they lock the doors.
I don't know why the hell I ever came before.
I'm gonna pack my bags and call my Mom,
I'm gonna turn this camp all upside down.
I'm gonna smoke and drink and cuss like hell
The hell I will.
To hell with the whole damn camp,
And the counselors,
To hell with the whole damn camp,
I really mean it,
To hell with the whole damn camp,
And I'll repeat it,
To hell with the whole damn camp.

◆ *Grainne, Alabama, 1970s.*[22]

Section Two: Dealing with Authority

CHURCH

Children, as has already been shown, will try to fight against restrictions of all sorts—even those set in the name of a Higher Power. Perhaps the greatest act of rebellion for a child brought up in an organized religion is that of parodying the rules and beliefs of the religion:

Version One:

My name is Jesus the son of Joe.
Hello, hello, hello, hello.
My son is Jesus,
He is a fraud,
He thinks he's God,
He thinks he's God.

♦ *Tina, Bronx, New York, 1960s.*

Version Two:

My name is Jesus the son of God,
I've come to heal you and save your bod'.

♦ *Tappan, Connecticut, early 1960s.*[23]

(to the tune of "Rockin' Robin")

Nails in his hands,
Nails in his feet,
Don't hear nothin' but that rockin' sockin' beat,
Rockin' Jesus.

♦ *Tappan, Connecticut, learned at his Unitarian youth group in the late 1960s. Informant notes that there are dozens of other verses.*[24]

Familiar hymns can also become vehicles for subversive messages:

(to the tune of "Jesus Loves You")

Jesus hates you this I know
'Cause the Bible tells me so.
And on this we all agree,
Jesus hates you more than me.

(chorus)
Yes, Jesus hates you.
Yes, Jesus hates you.
Yes, Jesus hates you.
He told me so himself.

♦ *Author Weisskopf who learned it in college from Yoli, who learned it in Ann Arbor, Michigan, late 1970s. Yoli went on to become a divinity student.* [25]

(to the tune of "High in the Steeple Hangs a Bell")

High in the steeple hangs a knife,
Old Father Simon killed his wife.
Blood dripping down every day, every hour,
Blood dripping down from the knife in the tower.
Clang on the head,
Now you're dead.

♦ *Jim, St. Patrick's Parochial School, Bedford, New York, 1960s. The informant adds, "The interesting thing is that it was sung at a Catholic school, where everyone knew priests don't marry, yet it speaks of Old Father Simon killing his wife."* [26]

'Twas midnight on the ocean,
Not a streetcar was in sight.

And a barefoot boy with shoes on
Sat standing in the light.
As the organ peeled potatoes
And the choir rendered lard,
As the sexton wrang the dishtowel,
Someone set the church on fire!
"Holy smoke!" the preacher shouted,
And in the flight he lost his hair.
Now his head resembles heaven,
'Cause there is no parting there.

◆ *Mary, who learned this from her cousin in northern Wisconsin, 1950s.*[27]

CHAPTER SIX:

THE OUTSIDE: POLITICS AND HOLIDAYS

At first a child's world is circumscribed by home, then by home and playground, then by the local neighborhood. As the child grows, school is added to that world, then camp and whatever territory is included in family vacations. He or she is generally also exposed to organized religion of some sort and to the theological terrain that comes with it.

A hundred years ago, a child's world wasn't likely to grow much larger than the relatively small circle of home, village, and church, particularly in rural areas where people tended not to travel very much. Now, thanks to media such as television and radio, and to stories overheard from newspaper-reading adults, children are becoming aware of the outside world at a younger and younger age. Though this precocious knowledge of a wider world can be stimulating to the mind and imagination, it also forces children to contend with words and images with which they may not be quite ready to deal.

However, folklore is ready to come to the aid of those children who may feel overwhelmed by the outside world and all its strangeness, allowing them to turn adult fears and fancies into more manageable farces.

WAR

War, in particular, has left its imprint on the minds of children, and hence on the childhood folk rhyme scene. Children who are far too young to have experienced any major war are still singing rhymes dealing with places and events in World War II—and in even earlier wars:

Version One:

(To the tune of "Reveille.")

There's a soldier in the grass
With a bullet up his ass.
Get it out, get it out,
Like a good Girl Scout.

◆ *Tom Kidd, Florida, ca. 1970s. Similar versions are known by author Weisskopf, Brooklyn, New York, probably mid-1970s, and author Sherman, Bronx, New York, probably early 1970s.*

Version Two:

There's a _____ in the grass
With a bullet up his ass
Get it out, get it out,
Get it out, Boy Scout.

◆ *Kathy, Henry Harris Elementary School, Bayonne, New Jersey, ca. mid-1960s. The informant adds, "I never heard the word "soldier" substituted for the blank above; around here, it was usually a two-syllable racial epithet."*

Version Three:

There's a Nazi in the grass
With a machete up his ass.

Take it out, Girl Scout,
Take it out, take it out.

◆ *Alan, Florida, ca. 1960s.*

Version Four:

There's a monkey in the grass
With a bullet up his ass.
Stick it in, stick it out,
Would you like to be a Scout?
Yes or no?

◆ *Peter, Yonkers, New York, age ten, 1994. Also known to his sister,
Liana, age seventeen, also from Yonkers, and Colleen, age eleven,
from Hastings-on-Hudson. The informant added, and the others,
who were listening, agreed, that this rhyme was used as a counting-out rhyme. Although Peter was uncomfortable about saying
the "dirty" word in this rhyme, neither he nor Colleen seemed
aware (at least in front of adults) of the sexual connotations.[1]*

Children also may use such unlikely mediums as lullabies
to get across their messages:

Sleep, baby, sleep.
Your father drives a Jeep.
Your mother was a German spy.
She was shot by the F.B.I.,
Sleep, baby, sleep.

◆ *Jim, Bedford, New York, ca. early 1960s. The informant adds,
"Lots of remnants from WWII in my school days."[2]*

Wars, like any other historical happenings, are generally
relatively topical events in children's folklore. While there have
been some stray remnants of earlier wars recorded in children's

rhymes, fifty to sixty years seems to be the limit of a topical rhyme's "freshness." As a result, some fifty years after World War II, there are still a good many rhymes about featuring the names of World War II antagonists; the children may not always know exactly what roles these people played, but they emphatically know who were the villains.

(to be sung to the tune of "Colonel Bogey's March")

Hitler ... has only got one ball,
Goering ... has two but very small.
Himmler ... has something sim'lar,
And poor Goebbels has no balls at all.

◆ *Claire, Silver Spring, Maryland, ca. mid-1960s. Also known to JoAnn, Louisiana, ca. late 1960s, and Sue, Brooklyn, New York, ca. 1967-1975.*[3]

Version One:

Whistle while you work.
Hitler is a jerk.
Mussolini bit his weenie,
Now it doesn't work.

◆ *Jeanne, Pitman, New Jersey, pre-teen, ca. 1970s. The informant adds, "We certainly were aware of who Hitler was: the great villain with the little mustache" of World War II, but agrees that a child's time sense is highly flexible; she was aware that her parents had lived through the war, but that war also seemed a long time ago. A similar version, substituting "pulled" for "bit" was collected from Tappan, ca. 1960s, Florida, from Darryl, ca. 1970s, Philadelphia, Pennsylvania, substituting "but" for "now" in the last line. Another version from Sue, Brooklyn, New York, ca. 1967-1975, concludes, "Now it doesn't squirt."*

Version Two:

Whistle while you work,
Hitler was a jerk.
Mussolini cut off his weenie,
Now it doesn't work.

◆ *Austin, Fort Worth, Texas, age ten in 1981-1982.*

Version Three:

Whistle while you work,
Mussolini bought a shirt,
Hitler wore it,
Britain tore it,
Whistle while you work.

◆ *Peter, who learned it from his father-in-law, who heard it during World War II, Halifax, Nova Scotia, Canada.*

Version Four:

Whistle while you work,
Hitler is a jerk.
Mussolini is a meany
And the Japs are worse.

◆ *Evelyn, Bronx, New York, circa late 1940s.*[4]

Another verse, set to a different tune, also features Mussolini.

Mussolini was a meanie and we're happy to say,
He lived in Italy all of his day.
We don't want him, you can have him,
He's too mean for us—

He's too mean, he's too mean, he's too mean, for us!

◆ *Caroline, Huntsville, Alabama, late 1970s.*

Version One:

(to "My Country 'Tis of Thee"/ "God Save the Queen")

My country's tired of me,
I'm going to Germany
To see the king.

His name is Donald Duck.
He drives a garbage truck.
So come along with me
To Germany.

◆ *Hank, Benham, Kentucky, ca. 1957-59.*

Version Two:

My country 'tis of thee
Sweet land of Germany
My name is Fritz.

My father was a spy.
Caught by the F.B.I.
Hung by his purple tie.
Isn't that the pits?

◆ *Lynn, Willingsboro, New Jersey, ca. mid-1960s.*

Version Three:

My country 'tis of thee,
I live in Germany,
My name is Schultz.
My father was a spy

Caught by the F.B.I.
Hung by his own necktie,
I wonder why.

◆ *Alan, Boston area, Massachusetts, ca. 1950s.*[5]

As new world leaders come into power, children's rhymes change to include these leaders. While children might not have understood all the ramifications of the Cold War, they certainly picked up ideas about the situation from their parents, teachers, and the media. But parodying these ideas wasn't necessarily the point; parodying authority in general was:

Version One:

(to the tune of "Casey Jones," which was used for
the "Good 'n' Plenty" jingle about Choo-Choo Charlie)

Once upon a time there was an engineer.
Fidel Castro was his name, we hear.
He ran his country and he sure had fun,
He used guns and ammunition to make his country run.
Khruschev says, "Love that Fidel Castro."
Khrushchev says, "He really rings the bell."
Khrushchev says, "Love that Fidel Castro.
If you don't love Castro, you will go to hell."

◆ *Leslie, early grade school, New York City, ca. 1960s.*

Version Two:

Once upon a time there was a Cuban queer.
Fidel Castro was his name we hear.
Making revolutions and he sure had fun
Using bullets and machine guns
To make the people run.
Castro says:

"Love that Mr. Khrushchev!"
Castro says:
"Love that Mr. K."
Castro says:
"Love that Mr. Khrushchev,
'Cause he's gonna drop an A-bomb
On the U.S.A."

◆ *Tappan, Florida, ca. 1960s. The informant adds, tongue-in-cheek, "There were so many of these anti-Castro, anti-Khrushchev and anti-Kennedy jingles floating around north Florida in the early '60s that I suspect there was a bureau of the CIA dedicated to inventing them and teaching them to school children."*[6]

(to the tune of the "Mickey Mouse Club March")

Who's the leader of the cult of personality?
M-A-O-T-S-E-DASH-T-U-N-G!
Mao Tse Tung!
(Mu Sho Chi!)
Mao Tse Tung!
(Cho En Lai!)
Forever let us hold our banners high!
Come along and sing the song and join the bureaucracy!
M-A-O-T-S-E-DASH-T-U-N-G!

◆ *Cory, Toronto, Canada, late 1970s.*

(to the tune of "Waltzing Matilda")

Courting the bour-jwah,
Courting the bour-jwah,
They come a-courtin' the bourgeois.
Ever since the day that Papa Stalin
Told 'em all to fall in,
They come a-courtin' the bourgeois.

Leon Trotsky was a Nazi
'Till they signed the Stalin-Hitler pact!

◆ *Cory, Toronto, Canada, late 1970s. The informant adds about this and the previous song, "Honest, these are kiddy songs—my folks are Reds." Pronunciations are from informant.*[7]

Sometimes a children's parody can be dated to a specific event. In 1962, the United States and the then-Soviet Union came perilously close to war over the missiles placed by the latter in Cuba. The crisis ended peacefully, but a good deal of adult panic filtered down to children, who countered with such parodies as the latter:

(to the tune of "Peter Cottontail")

Here comes Khrushchev Cotton-tail
Hopping down the Missile trail.
Hippity, hoppity, war is on its way ...

◆ *Greg, Connecticut, 1962.*[8]

(to the tune of "Havah Nagila")

Hava-na Cuba, Hava-na Cuba, Hava-na Cuba,
That's where Castro's at!
Rockets and bombs and planes,
Miss-iles and other things.
In the land where I was born,
Russians, Go Home.

◆ *Dan, West Virginia, ca. 1960s.*[9]

While children are, on the whole, only vaguely aware of politics, they do learn about political parties and the names of

Section Two: Dealing with Authority

major political figures from their parents, teachers, and the media:

> The election is over.
> The winner is known.
> The will of the people
> Has clearly been shown.
>
> The battle's behind us;
> It's all in the past.
> So I'll hug your elephant,
> And you kiss my ass.

◆ *Dan, Charleston, West Virginia, ca. 1950s.*[10]

Children's rhymes of the outside world don't merely reflect political events and upheavals. They also indicate changing social mores, particularly where relations between different races are concerned, as one well-known counting-out rhyme indicates:

Version One:

> Eeny meeny miney moe,
> Catch a nigger by the toe.
> If he hollers
> Let him go.
> My mother said so.

◆ *Jim, Pennsylvania, ca. 1940s; also Mary Ellen, Birmingham, Alabama, late 1940s.*

Version Two:

> Eeny meeny, miney moe,
> Catch a robber by the toe.
> Don't you holler,

Don't you cry.
Just call the local F.B.I.

◆ *Andy, Brooklyn, New York, late 1960s.*

Version Three:

Eenie, meenie, minee-mo,
Catch a tiger by the toe.
If he hollers, let him go.
Eenie, meenie, minee-mo.
My mother said to pick the very best one and you are not IT.

◆ *Elissa, Syracuse, New York, ca. 1960s.*

Version Four:

Eeny Meeny Miney Mo,
Catch a tiger by the toe.
If he hollers, let him go.
He wanted a cookie but his mother said no.

(to be followed with:)
My mother said to
Pick a peach, pick a plum,
Pick a stick of chewing gum.

◆ *Claire, Silver Spring, Maryland, ca. 1960s. The informant adds, "Now, when my mother first heard me recite 'Eeny Meeny Miney Mo,' she was shocked. She had me repeat it, and enunciate every word very carefully. And then she wouldn't tell me why it bothered her. A few years later, she told me ... that the original words ... were, 'Catch a nigger by the toe,' and she was ... disturbed to hear that sort of racist rhyme was going through the neighborhood, until she realized that it had become completely transmuted—no child in the neighborhood had any inkling that it had ever referred to anything other than a tiger, although we all realized that the phrase, 'Catch a tiger by the toe,' didn't make much sense, but then, a lot of our rhymes didn't make sense."*

Version Five:

Eeny Meeny Miney Mo,
Catch a tiger by the toe.
If he hollers, let him go.
Eeny meeny miney moe.

My mother and your mother were hanging out clothes.
My mother socked your mother right in the nose.
What color was the blood?
R-e-d spells red, and you are not it.

◆ *Caroline, Huntsville, Alabama, 1970s. Informant was also familiar with the "nigger" variant, and another, "redneck."*[11]

But mores don't change completely very quickly. The following is an example of the type of vicious rhyme extant during the racial unrest of the 1960s:

(to the tune of the "Oscar Mayer Wiener" commercial jingle)

I wish I were an Alabama trooper.
That is what I truly wish to be,
'Cause if I were an Alabama trooper,
Then I could shoot the niggers legally.

◆ *J.M., Westchester, New York, 1965. The informant, who wished to remain anonymous and who emphatically does not believe in the sentiments in the rhyme, adds, "I doubt the kids who sang it had ever seen a real, live black person."*[12]

Children also may become aware as they mature of other forms of social conflict and injustice, such as unjust arrest, or the arrest of (implied) vagrants for loitering. Some of these rhymes clearly reflect earlier times in this country, with references to "paddy wagons" and such, while others lose the element of social complaint somewhere in the transmittal from one child to the next. But even those children who have no idea what those social references mean can still enjoy the weird image of insects playing that quintessentially American game, baseball:

Version One:

Standing on the corner,
Doing no one harm.
Along comes a copper,
Grabs me by the arm.
Drags me around the corner,
Rings a funny bell.
Along comes a paddy wagon,
Takes me to my cell.

I lay in my cell,
Looking at the wall.
Some bedbugs and cockroaches
Are having a game of ball.
The score is six to nothing,
The cockroaches are ahead,
A bedbug hits a homer,
And knocks me out of bed.

◆ *Karen, who learned this rhyme from her father in Chicago, age forty-two, 1994.*

Version Two:

I woke up one fine morning
And stepped upon a nail.
A policeman came and saw me
And took me off to jail.
In jail they serve you coffee,
In jail they serve you tea,

Sherman & Weisskopf

In jail they serve you everything
Except that darn old key.

I woke up one fine morning
And looked up on the wall.
The cooties and the bedbugs
Were having a game of ball.
The score was six to nothing.
The cooties were ahead.
The bedbugs hit a home run
And knocked me out of bed.

◆ *Claire, Silver Spring, Maryland, late 1960s.*

Version Three:

I woke up Monday morning,
I looked across my wall.
The skeeters and the bedbugs were playing a game of ball.
The score was nineteen-twenty,
The skeeters were ahead.
The bedbugs hit a homer and knocked me out of bed.

◆ *John, first or second grade, Detroit area, ca. early 1960s. The informant adds, "As I recall, kids on a bus can sing that one over and over until the driver goes berserk and does something tabloid-worthy."*[13]

HOLIDAYS

Perhaps the number one holiday to be parodied by children is Christmas. While the children aren't making fun of basic religious tenets, they certainly do react to the overdose of familiar carols heard on all fronts:

Version One:

(to be sung to the tune of "We Three Kings of Orient Are")

We three kings of Orient are
Chewing on a rubber cigar.
It was loaded
And exploded,
Blowing us all to kingdom come.

◆ *Bruce, Phoenix, New York, late 1950s.*

Version Two:

We three Kings of Orient are
Smoking on a rubber cigar.
Cigar was loaded, it exploded. BOOM!
Silent night, holy night.

◆ *Jim, Connecticut, ca. 1970s. Also known to Meg, Van Nuys, California, ca. 1951-1952, "MoorHardi," Louisville, Kentucky, ca. 1972, and Kevin, Idaho, age ten, 1978.*

Version Three:

We three kings of Orient are
Smoking on a rubber cigar.
Cigar was loaded,
It exploded.

We two kings of Orient are
Smoking on a rubber cigar.
Cigar was loaded,
It exploded.

We one king of Orient are
Smoking on a rubber cigar.
Cigar was loaded,
It exploded.

God rest ye, merry gentlemen.

◆ *Author Sherman, who learned this version in the early 1980s from Corinna, probably in her late teens, and her mother, Perdita, both from Brooklyn, New York. Also known to Lindalee, who learned it at Brownie day camp, Manitowoc, Wisconsin, ca. 1959-60.*[14]

Version One:

Jingle Bells,
Shotgun shells,
Santa Claus is dead.
Rudolph took a .22
And shot him in the head.

◆ *Randy, mid-Michigan, age twelve or thirteen, 1978-1979. An other wise identical version from Claire, Silver Spring, Maryland, ca. 1960s, substitutes "someone" for "Rudolph."*

Version Two:

Jingle Bells,
Santa smells,
A million miles away.
Stuffed his nose
With Cheerios
And ate them all the way—hey!

◆ *Katzi, third grade at Colebrook Elementary School, New Hampshire, age nine, 1994. Similarly Sue, Brooklyn, New York, ca. 1967-75.*

Version Three:

Jingle Bells,
Rudolph smells,
Santa ran away.
Oh what fun it is to ride

In his stinky Chevrolet.

◆ *Lynn, Willingboro, New Jersey, ca. mid-1960s. Also known to Claire, Silver Spring, Maryland, ca. 1960s.*

Version Four:

Jungle bells,
Santa smells,
Easter's on its way,
Oh what fun it is to ride
In a beat-up Chevrolet-ay!

◆ *Kathy, Henry Harris Elementary School, Bayonne, New Jersey, mid-1960s.*

Version Five:

Jingle bells,
Santa smells,
Happy Halloween.
Oh what fun it is to ride
In a German submarine.

Jingle bells,
Santa smells,
Happy Halloween.
Oh what fun it is to ride
In a Nazi submarine.

◆ *Meryle, Menlo Park, New Jersey, 1968.*

Version Six:

Jingle Bells,
Shock and shells.
Bee-bees in the air.
Oh what fun it is to ride

In Santa's underwear!

◆ *Jim, Connecticut, ca. 1970s. The informant notes that other names may be inserted in place of Santa Claus, and that another favorite substitution was "Grandma."*[15]

Familiar melodies are not the only source of material for parodies. Famous poems often become the victims of children's parodies as well:

> 'Twas the night before Christmas and all through the garage,
> Not a creature was stirring, not even the Dodge.
> The tires were hung by the chimney with care
> In hopes that St. Nicholas would fill them with air.

◆ *Jim, Connecticut, ca. 1970s.*[16]

Version One:

(to the tune of "Rudolph the Red-Nosed Reindeer")

> Randolph the bow-legged cowboy
> Had a very shiny gun.
> And if you ever saw it,
> It would surely make you run.
> All of the other cowboys
> Used to laugh and call him names.
> They never let poor Randolph
> Join in any cowboy games.
> Then one foggy Christmas Eve
> The sheriff came to say,
> "Randolph with your gun so bright,
> Won't you shoot my wife tonight?"
> Then how the cowboys loved him
> As they shouted out with glee,

"Randolph the bow-legged cowboy,
You'll go to the penitentiary!"

◆ *Author Sherman, New York City, late 1960s-early 1970s. An
almost identical version was collected from Andrea, Fairvalley
School, Covina, California, ca. 1964-1965; this version ends,
"You'll go down in history." Another almost identical version
from Hank, Benham, Kentucky, ca. 1950s, began, "Rudolph the
red-nosed cowboy."*

Version Two:

Then all the other cowboys,
Laughed and shouted out with glee,
"Mav'rick the Lonely Cowboy,
We'll hang you from the highest tree."

◆ *Jim, St. Patrick's Parochial School, Bedford, New York, ca.
1960s.*[17]

    Halloween, that supreme candy-getting and costume-wear-
ing holiday beloved by children, also has a widespread children's parody:

Version One:

Trick-or-treat,
Smell my feet,
Give me something good to eat.
If you don't,
I don't care,
I'll make you eat your underwear!

◆ *Judy, Michigan, ca. 1970s.*

Version Two:

Trick or treat,

Smell my feet,
Give me something good to eat.
If you don't,
I don't care.
I'll pull down your underwear.

◆ *Lucy Rose, Little Rock, Arkansas, age six, 1992.*[18]

A less frequently parodied holiday is Groundhog Day. But we have collected at least one children's rhyme in celebration of this more obscure holiday:

Joy to the world, the groundhog's dead.
We barbecued his head.
What happened to his toes?
We shoved them up his nose.
What happened to his body?
We flushed it down the potty.
What happened to his feet?
We needed something to eat.
Joy to the world, the groundhog's dead.

◆ *Katzi, third grade, Colebrook Elementary School, Colebrook, New Hampshire, age nine, 1994.*[19]

SECTION THREE:

THE COMMERCIAL WORLD: THE MEDIUM IS THE MESSAGE

Humans have been telling essentially the same jokes since the beginning of recorded history. This is, of course, what makes jokes folklore and not literature. Jokes commonly thought of as new, or even topical, are for the most part old jokes recycled with new names inserted.[1] The same is true of ditties based on advertising tunes, television shows, and popular songs. Very rarely is the butt of the parody the product advertised or the television show itself; most often, new verses making use of new tunes explore the same themes, violate the same taboos, even repeat the same lines.

Nevertheless, as the line separating the personal and the public, the home and the commercial world, becomes ever more tenuous, the commercial world is increasingly the springboard for folklore. Advertising, television shows, and popular songs heard on the radio and video TV are the shared culture of the masses in America and as far across the world as American television programs penetrate. It is reassuring that, rather than consume this commercial culture uncritically, children engage in the widespread and lively folk parody sampled in this section.[2] In these verses, it is not just a familiar tune that is appropriated to communicate children's folklore: the folklore itself is about the tune.

CHAPTER SEVEN:

ADVERTISING FOLLIES

One may feel a slight twinge of conscience at hearing "The Battle Hymn of the Republic" twisted into an assault on teachers or "Joy to the World" contorted into a paean to violence, but it's hard to feel bad when an advertising jingle is appropriated and revised in a clever manner. While advertising parodies and other uses of advertising tunes tend to be less enduring than other kinds of ditties included in this volume, some have a longevity outlasting the advertisements on which they were based. This may be in part because advertising jingles are composed to be memorable, intended to resonate in the brains of the listeners.

As advertising becomes ever more a part of everyday life (every hour, every place ...), and increasingly targeted toward children, it becomes itself an institution to be mocked, an authority to be questioned. Some of the most popular companies in the U.S. make the sweetest targets (partially because the biggest companies can afford writers of the catchiest jingles and saturation marketing). Thus, parodies of commercials combine the traditional pleasures of gross-outs and the breaking of sexual and bodily function taboos with the pleasure of subversive imitation, thus contributing to their continued existence in children's folklore.[1]

FOOD

One of the largest franchises in the world is a chain of hamburger joints found under the golden arches—McDonald's restaurants:

Restaurants

Version One:

("to the old McDonald's theme")

McDonald's is your kind of place *(clap, clap!)*
Hamburgers in your face *(clap, clap!)*
French fries up your nose *(clap, clap!)*
Pickles between your toes,
And special sauce in your face,
Big Macs all over the place,
McDonald's is your kind of place!

◆ *Lynn, Willingboro, New Jersey, ca. mid-1960s.*

Version Two:

McDonald's is your kind of place,
Hamburgers smashed in your face,
French fries up your nose,
Pickles between your toes.

Before you get your money back,
You'll have a heart attack,
McDonald's is your kind of place.

◆ *John, Portland, Oregon, ca. 1970.*

Version Three:

McDonald's is your kind of place.
There is no parking space.
French fries up your nose,
Ketchup between your toes.

◆ *Laura Ann, learned from her older sister, Suzanne, central New Jersey, ca. mid-1970s.*

Version Four:

McDonald's was our kind of place
Until they/we burnt it down.
They/we burnt it to the ground.
They/we even burnt the clown.
McDonald's was our kind of place,
Oh, what a crappy place,
McDonald's was our kind of place.

◆ *Sue, Brooklyn, New York, ca. 1967-75.*

Version Five:

McDonald's is your kind of place,
It's such a happy place.
Ham-boogers up your nose,
French fries between your toes,
And don't forget our chocolate shakes
Made from polluted lakes.
McDonald's is your kind of place,
Our kind of place.

◆ *Grainne, Alabama, ca. 1970s. A similar version was collected from JoAnn, Louisiana, ca. early 1960s.*

Version Six:

McDonald's is your kind of place!

Hamburgers in your face!
French fries between your toes,
Pickles right up your nose!
Last time that I ate there,
They gave me underwear.
McDonald's is your kind of place!

◆ *Caroline, Huntsville, Alabama, ca. early 1970s.*

Version Seven:

McDonald's is your kind of place.
Hamburgers in your face,
French Fries up your nose,
Hot Dogs between your toes.
McDonald's is your kind of place.

◆ *Hal, Virginia, ca. 1980s. A similar version was collected from
Mitch, Brooklyn, New York, ca. 1960s.[2]*

That wasn't the only McDonald's ad to come in for it.
Here are two others:

Version One:

You deserve a break today,
So go out and break a leg
At McDonald's!

◆ *Lynn, Willingboro, New Jersey, ca. mid-1960s.*

Version Two:

When you've just flunked a test,
You're not feeling your best,
Take a trip down the stairs,
Leave your worries and cares,

You deserve ptomaine today
So get up and get away
To the kitchen,
They do it all to you.

◆ *Informant Jim, learned at high school in White Plains, New York,
from about 1970.*

Since many a teenager has worked in fast food restaurants,
it is not surprising that a retaliatory rhyme should come into
being:

Version Three:

With a bucket and mop
(doot, do do do do),
We clean up all the slop
(doot, do do do do),
From the triple thick shakes
And the french fries you've dropped.

We deserve a break today
So get out and stay away
From McDona-a-a-a-lds!

◆ *Dan, Charleston, West Virginia, 1970s.*

McDonald's isn't alone in being the target of children's
parodies; its rival, Burger King, also comes in for some jesting:

Hold the pickle, hold the lettuce,
Shut up, lady, you upset us.
All we ask is that you let us
Do it our way.
Do it our way
Or go to Burger King.

◆ *Laura Ann, central New Jersey, ca. mid-1970s.*[3]

Local restaurants with hyperbolic claims can also be the target of parody:

Everybody goes to Gino's
'Cause Gino's is the place to go,
Everybody goes to Gino's,
Everybody in the know.
The most rewarding flavor in this man's world
For people who are having fun,
Schaefer is the one beer to have
When you're having more than one!

◆ *Lynn, Willingboro, New Jersey, ca. mid-1960s. Informant explains: "There was also the combined Gino's/Schaefer Beer jingle we used to sing on the bus. The two jingles, in their respective commercials, were kind of incomplete. The first one didn't really have an ending; the second showed up at the end of the ad. They were both in the same key, same meter, and sounded VERY similar. The appended jingles came out like this: (above)."*

Pre-prepared Food

With the advent of the age of the working mother, time-saving foods became more common on America's dinner table. Some gained more acceptance with sensitive children's palates than others. In the 1960s, Chef Boyardee ran a commercial for its canned Beefaroni that was widely parodied:

Version One:

Hooray for Beefaroni,
It's made from macaroni.

Beefaroni's really neat,
It makes you throw up in the street.
Hooray—for Beefaroni!

◆ *Lynn, Willingboro, New Jersey, ca. mid-1960s.*

Version Two:

We're having horse manure,
We found it in the sewer.
Horse manure's really neat,
Horse manure's is nice and sweet,
Horse manure's a real treat,
Hooray! For horse manure.

◆ *Claire, Maryland, mid-1960s: "We had an alternate line that we would often substitute for one of the three consecutive rhymes: 'Makes you throw up in the street.' " Informant also notes: "It seems like we were always lampooning commercials. In this ditty, 'manure' is often pronounced with three syllables, as man-oo-re." Similar versions were collected from Jim, White Plains, New York, ca. 1964, and Mitch, Brooklyn, New York, ca. 1960s.[4]*

Ricearoni, another convenience food, also had an ubiquitous ad:

Ricearoni, the San Francisco treat
Ricearoni, it's stuff you just can't eat ....
Started out where cablecars sing this song
Now throw it away or you won't last long,
Ricearoni, the San Francisco treat.

◆ *Jim, White Plains, New York, 1965 or 1966.*

The following parody of the Oscar Mayer Wiener ad of the mid-1960s is the exception to the rule that rhymes based on advertising parody the product advertised:

> I wish I were a three-legged doggy
> That is what I'd truly like to be
> For if I were a three-legged doggy,
> I wouldn't have to lift my leg to pee.

◆ *Sheryl, Connecticut, ca. late 1970s, "But I'd guess it's been around longer."*[5]

This ditty, which is a parody, changes ever so slightly the wording of an original commercial run from the early 1970s:

> If you think it's butter, but it's snot,
> It's Chiffon.

◆ *Author Weisskopf, Brooklyn, New York, early 1970s.* [6]

Sweets

Children buy candy, therefore candy has always been marketed with an eye toward children. But even though children may not be able to resist sweets, they certainly can prove resilient to the lure of advertising:

> N-E-S-T-L-E-S—
> Cram it up your ass
> Sideways!

◆ *Jan, who learned from her older sister in Washington, D.C., eight years old, 1960.*[7]

> Bungalow Bar
> Tastes like tar;

The more you eat it
The sicker you are.

◆ *Lisa, P.S. 96, Bronx, New York, sixth grade, 1966.*[8]

("to the tune of The Tootsie Roll Song")

Choc-choc-choclatey,
Chew-chew-chewy ...
JUNIOR, PUT THAT BACK IN THE TOILET!

◆ *Denia, California, late 1960s.*[9]

Drink

Cola and beer commercials being some of the most ubiquitous ads found these days, it's surprising that so very few of the rhymes we collected dealt with these beverages. Perhaps that's because they no longer rely so heavily on easily parodied ditties, but rather on a series of images, MTV-style.[10]

From an earlier age, however, we find a cola parody:

Version One:

Pepsi Cola hits the spot,
Twelve full ounces, that's a lot.
Take a sip and throw it down,
Then go buy a Royal Crown.

◆ *Jerry, Tennessee, ca. 1940s.*

Version Two:

Pepsi Cola hits the spot,
Ties your stomach in a knot.
Pepsi Cola tastes like ink,

Pepsi Cola is a lousy/rotten drink.

◆ *Author Sherman, Bronx, New York, ca. late-1960s. The informant notes that the choice of "lousy" or "rotten" in the last line depended on the mood of the singer.*[11]

Not all parodies of advertisements are of national brands. But that doesn't make them any less stinging:

Byrne Dairy milk is mighty fine,
It tastes just like turpentine.
If you drink too much of it,
You will soon get sick of it.

◆ *Elissa, Syracuse, New York, ca. 1960s; learned from a friend in the second or third grade.*[12]

ADULT PLEASURES

Making fun of adult things makes one seem more sophisticated, or so the logic of these parodies seems to run. In the parodies of cigarettes below, the implication is that those reciting have themselves tried cigarettes and are so sophisticated as to be able to judge a cigarette's quality:

Version One:

Winston tastes bad, like the one I just had.
No filter, no flavor, tastes like toilet paper.

◆ *Rod, age eight, Linwood, California, early 1960s. Also contributed by Claire, mid-1960s, Maryland.*

Section Three: The Commercial World

Version Two:

Winston tastes bad, like the one I first had,
No filter, no flavor, tastes like used toilet paper.

◆ *Tim, Walnut Creek, California, 1967-68.*

Version Three:

Winston tastes bad like the one I just had.
No filter, no blend, 'cause I smoked the wrong end.

◆ *Mitch, Brooklyn, 1960s.*

Version Four:

Winston tastes bad like the last one I had.
No filter, no taste, just a thirty-cent waste.

◆ *Denia, California, late 1960s. Informant notes: "Catch the price!"*

Version Five:

Winston tastes good,
Like a Prime Minister should.

◆ *Hank, Benham, Kentucky, 1957-60.*[13]

Similar to the verses above, the implication in this next one is that the versifier and her listeners drink beer—indeed, they already have an allegiance to a particular brand!

Mary Margaret Truman was the daughter of the pres.
She lived up in the White House with her ugly mother, Bess.
She went to Missouri and started a brewery,
So let's all switch to Schlitz.

◆ *Denia, California, late 1960s. Possibly to the tune of "The*

Missouri Waltz" informant notes. Informant also remembers this conversation when overheard reciting this rhyme and others: "Mother: 'I don't think those are very nice. Don't teach them to your little sister!' Toooo late."[14]

One of the great adult privileges is owning a car, that symbol of the ultimate American freedom: the ability to take off at any time and go anywhere. But if you are not yet old enough to drive, you can at least make fun of the commercials:

Buy a Ford, buy a Ford,
Buy a Ford today.
If you can't afford a Ford,
Buy a Chevrolet ...

◆ *Tappan, Florida, ca. 1960s.*

Most children can't simply pack up and take a vacation at will. Spoiling the illusions of those who can is the next best thing:

Come back to Jamaica,
We'll hi-jack your plane.
We'll steal all your luggage
And sell you cocaine.

◆ *Jennifer, Bronx, New York, 1970s.*[15]

CLEANING PRODUCTS

Why do children parody ads of cleaning products so often, when presumably they'd have no interest in buying or using such things? Probably because cleaning products are traditionally widely advertised on daytime television, and perhaps because mothers harp on restrictions about handling and ingesting dangerous cleaning substances.[16]

By far the most widely found parody we uncovered was that of a Comet commercial utilizing the tune of the theme song from the movie *The Bridge on the River Kwai*, "The Colonel Bogey March:"[17]

Version One:

Comet, it tastes like gasoline.
Comet, it makes your teeth turn green.
Comet, it makes you vomit,
So get some Comet and vomit today.

◆ *Claire, Maryland, mid-1960s. Similarly Tom, Texas and Florida, early 1960s; Kathy, Henry Harris Elementary School, Bayonne, New Jersey, ca. mid-1960s; Beth, central Ohio, 1955-1960. Marla learned a variant as a young teen in a New York City area camp between 1980 and 1983 that began, "Comet, it makes your mouth turn green ..." Frankie, Bronx, New York, ca. late 1970s, had a variant that began, "Comet, it makes your dick turn green. / Comet, it makes you smell like gasoline ...."*

Version Two:

Comet tastes like Listerine,
Comet will make your eyes turn green.
Comet tastes like vomit,
So eat Comet and vomit today!

◆ *Tom, Nebraska, ca. 1970s.*

Version Three:

Comet, it makes your teeth turn red.
Comet, it makes you wet your bed.
Comet, it will make you vomit,

So buy some Comet and vomit today.

◆ *Karen, Fort Worth, Texas, ca. 1967.*[18]

An extremely local version is known to author Weisskopf, learned in Brooklyn, Flatbush, early 1970s:

Version Four:

Rejex, they make your feet feel fine,
Rejex, they cost a dollar ninety nine,
Rejex, I love my Rejex,
So buy your Rejex ... today. [19]

"The Colonel Bogey March" provided the tune for other children's rhymes as well:

Version Five:

Ajax, it makes your mouth turn blue.
Ajax, it tastes like Elmer's Glue.
Ajax, will make you pay tax,
So buy some Ajax, and pay tax, today.

◆ *Marla, learned as a young teen in a New York City area camp between 1980 and 1983.*[20]

Ajax, a rival brand of all purpose cleaner to Comet, comes in for a share of the abuse, including verses taking off from its own commercials:

(to be sung to the Ajax commercial jingle)

Drink Ajax
(boom boom)
The Foamin' Cleanser.

Watch your teeth
Go down the drain.
(bo bo bo bo bo bo boom)

◆ *Dan, Charleston, West Virginia, ca. 1950s. The informant adds,*
"I loved this one when my voice changed and I could do the deep
booms."

Mess up your shirt,
Mess up your shirt,
New Ajax Laundry Detergent
Will mess up your shirt.

◆ *Jim, White Plains, New York, 1962 or 1963.*[21]

Another product designed to make things whiter and
brighter, this time teeth, is an easy target:

Version One:

You'll wonder where the yellow went
When you brush your teeth with white cement.

◆ *Jim who learned it from his sister: "who was in first grade at Our*
Lady of Good Council in White Plains, New York at the time
(ca. 1959). The place was run by the Sisters of the Divine
Compassion, who were known by their little charges (out of
earshot) as Sisters of the Blind Retribution."

Version Two:

You'll wonder where the enamel went
When you brush your teeth with wet cement.
WEEEEEET CEMEEEEEEENNNNNTTTT!

◆ *Cat, New Jersey, mid-1960s.*

Version Three:

You'll wonder where your teeth all went
When you brush your teeth with Pepsodent.

◆ *Author Sherman, Bronx, New York, ca. 1960s.*[22]

Finally, one verse that sums up the entire commercial world up:

As I was walking down the street
One dark and dreary day,
I came upon a billboard,
And much to my dismay,
The sign was torn and tattered
From the rain the night before.
The wind and rain had done its job
For this is what I saw:

Smoke Coca-Cola cigarettes,
Chew Wrigley's spearmint beer,
Ken-L-Ration dog food
Makes your wife's complexion clear.
Simonize your baby
In a Hershey's candy bar,
And Texaco's the beauty cream
That's used by all the stars.
So take your next vacation
In a brand new Frigidaire.
Learn to play the piano
In your grandma's underwear.
Doctors say that babies
Should smoke till they are three.
And people over sixty-five
Should bathe in Lipton Tea (in flow-thru teabags).

◆ *Elizabeth, at Camp Reily, Harrisburg, Pennsylvania, 1978.*[23]

CHAPTER EIGHT:

TELEVISION, SUPERHEROES, AND SONGS WE ALL KNOW

In the process of creating folk rhymes, tunes are commandeered, appropriated, and otherwise used shamelessly to carry the lyrics of songs never previously associated with that music. A good many American folk songs that have different words from the originals from the Old Country. The sturdy tunes endured, but the lyrics evolved with the eras.[1] So subversive rhymes of children that take commonly known tunes and meld them into verses more interesting to young sensibilities are in keeping with a long-standing folk tradition.

Humans have any number of ways of indicating "tribal" membership, from ritual scarification of young men to the use of technical jargon within a work group. And kids are continually reinventing slang in order to exclude the old, the "cool" of yesteryear replaced by the "phat" of yesterday. But another way to exclude age cohorts is to make fun of their popular entertainment—or one's own, excluding those who are not familiar with the object of mockery. Thus, sometimes the original song itself is the object of parody. The purpose of the rhyme is not to gross-out peers or explore sexual or body taboos, but to overtly tear down cultural icons. And in modern times, the cultural icons shared by all are transmitted via the airwaves through TV and radio.

TELEVISION

Any TV show intended to be watched by children or "the family" is especially vulnerable to parody, since they are targeted toward those who create subversive rhymes. Below are two versions of subversive rhymes easily adapted to mock different icons:[2]

Version One:

On top of Old Smokey,
All covered with hair,
I saw Betty Grable
Kiss Dr. Kildare.

◆ *Tappan, Florida, ca. 1960s.*

Version Two:

On top of Old Smokey,
All covered with snow,
I saw Roy Rogers
Screw Marilyn Monroe.

He took off his pants
And hung them on a stick.
She said, oh you have
Such a great big *(slight pause)* horse.
He said, my gosh, ma'am,
You sure do look pretty.
Then he lay down beside her
And played with her (slight pause) toes.

("One more verse I can't remember in which the passion is consummated.")

On top of Old Smokey,

All covered with snow,
I saw Roy Rogers
Screw Marilyn Monroe.

◆ *Hank, Benham, Kentucky, 1958-59, and on later occasions. Informant notes that "screw" in the last line of the first verse can be replaced by "f___," that "horse" in the last line of the second verse can be replaced by "gun," and that "I've also heard this with Gene Autry in place of Roy Rogers and Bridget Bardot in place of Marilyn Monroe."[3]*

The cartoon hero Popeye has had a long time to inspire ditties parodying his own signature tune:

Version One:

I'm Popeye the sailor man,
I live in a garbage can.
I eat all the worms
And spit out the germs,
I'm Popeye the sailor man.

I'm Popeye the sailor man,
I'm Popeye the sailor man.
I hate to go swimming
With bald-headed women,
I'm Popeye the sailor man.

◆ *Hank, Benham, Kentucky, heard ca. 1957-58.*

Version Two:

I'm Popeye the Sailor Man,
I live in a garbage can.
I eat all the worms and I spit out the germs,

I'm Popeye the Sailor Man, toot, toot.

◆ *Jim, Connecticut, 1960s, similarly Denia, California, mid 1960s, and Gayle, who notes, "My kids used to sing that one ... at the top of their lungs, when they were in the swimming pool ... or from the diving board (using it as a stage) ..." A version from Kathy, Henry Harris Elementary School, Bayonne, New Jersey, ca. mid-1960s, includes the line, "I eat all the junk and I smell like a skunk," while a version from Elissa, Syracuse, New York, ca. 1960s, includes the line "I eat all the worms and get all the germs."[4]*

Astro Boy was a cartoon of the early 1960s, like *Popeye* featuring a theme song and a hero—practically an invitation to parody!

Astroboy in your flight,
You just spoiled my appetite.
As a hero, you're a zero,
As you fight, fight, fight,
Astroboy.

◆ *Jim, St. Patrick's Parochial School, Bedford, New York, early 1960s.[5]*

In Walt Disney's live-action show *Davy Crockett*, a real historical character was taken and elevated to the status of hero:

(to the tune "The Ballad of Davy Crockett")

Version One:

Born on a tabletop in Joe's cafe,
Dirtiest place in the USA,
Shot his father with a three-oh-three,
Polished off his mother with DDT.

Davy, Davy Crockett,
King of the Wild Frontier.

◆ *Jim, St. Patrick's Parochial School, Bedford, New York, early 1960s.*

Version Two:

Born on a meteor from outer space,
Met a Martian face to face.
He's not afraid because he knows
You get Go-Power from Cheerios.
Davy, Davy Crockett,
King of the Wild Frontier.

◆ *Author Sherman, Bronx, New York, ca. 1960s.*

Version Three:

Born on a mountaintop in Palestine,
Raised on gefilte fish and Mogen David wine.
He was bar-mitzvahed when he was only nine,
His name wasn't Crockett, his name was Finklestein!
His name was Davy, Davy Finklestein,
King of the Wild Frontier!

◆ *Cory, Toronto, Ontario, Canada, ca. 1970s.*[6]

In *Branded*, a television western of the 1960s, the hero is a cowboy, like Crockett the frontiersman, a potent symbol of a virile young America. And again, the show also had a memorable theme song:

Version One:

(to the theme of Branded)

Stranded.

Stuck on the toilet bowl.
What do you do when you're stranded
And you don't have a roll?

◆ *Claire, Maryland, ca. mid-1960s.*

Version Two:

Stranded!
Stranded on a toilet bowl!
What can you do when you're stranded
And you don't have a roll?
You can prove you're a man
By resorting to your hand ...
STRANDED!

◆ *Adam, Honesdale, Pennsylvania, late 1960s. The informant also provided the following version:*

Version Three:

Stranded!
Stranded on a desert isle!
What can you do if you're stranded
And (name of person you hate)'s there for a while?
You can prove you're a man
By sockin' 'em with your hand ...
STRANDED!

◆ *Adam, Honesdale, Pennsylvania, late 1960s.*

Version Four:

He was innocent,
Not a charge was true,
But they hanged him anyway ...

◆ *Jim, St. Patrick's Parochial School, Bedford, New York, ca. 1960s.*

Section Three: The Commercial World

Version Five:

He was guilty,
Every charge was true,
But they let him get away ...

◆ *Jim, St. Patrick's Parochial School, Bedford, New York, ca. 1960s.*[7]

Howdy Doody wasn't a hero; he was a puppet, the star of one of the first and longest-lived television shows, running from the 1940s all the way to 1960:

(to the tune of "Ta-Ra-Ra-Boom-Der-Ay")

Version One:

It's Howdy Doody time, it isn't worth a dime,
So let's wash off their sign, and we'll watch Frankenstein.

◆ *Mary, San Francisco Bay area, California, 1980s.*

Version Two:

It's Howdy Doody Time.
The show's not worth a dime,
So turn to channel nine—
Watch Mr. Frankenstein.

◆ *Wendell, Ohio, learned in grade school in the late-1960s.*[8]

The *Addams Family* provided a different take on traditional home life for the children of the 1960s from other live-action wholesome family comedies like *Father Knows Best* and *The Donna Reed Show*: members of this nice extended family were literally monsters:

(to The Addams Family theme)

The Addams Family started
When Uncle Fester farted.
They all grew up retarded,
The Addams family.

◆ *Claire, Maryland, mid-1960s.*[9]

To the children of the Seventies, *The Brady Bunch*, starring Florence Henderson as the wife who attempted to combine two broken families, epitomized family life:

(to the theme of The Brady Bunch)

It's the story
Of an ugly lady,
Who was bringing up three very ugly girls.
All of them had purple hair
Like their mother,
The youngest one was bald.

It's the story of a man named Lady
Who was busy with three assholes of his own.
They were four jerks
Living all together,
Yet they were all alone.

Till the one day when the lady met this jello,
And they knew it was much more than a hunch,
So they screwed and formed up a family.
And that's the way they all became the neighbor's lunch.

The neighbor's lunch!
The neighbor's lunch!
That's they way they became the neighbor's lunch!

◆ *Cory, Toronto, Ontario, Canada, ca. 1970s.*[10]

Sesame Street, starring Big Bird and crew, first aired in 1969 and is still running. Like *Howdy Doody*, the TV show is aimed at children, but it provided much of America with the first portrayal of a multicultural, urban childhood that was as normal as suburban life. And it has a memorable theme song:

> Smoggy day,
> Ev'rything's dark and grey,
> Hostile neighbors shout,
> They're down and out!
> Can you tell me how to get,
> How to get to Reality Street?

♦ *Cory, Toronto, Ontario, Canada, ca. 1970s.*[11]

(to the tune of Sesame Street's *"People in Your Neighborhood")*

Version One:

> Oh the podiatrist is a person in your neighborhood,
> In your neighborhood,
> In your neighborhood,
> Oh the podiatrist is a person in your neighborhood.
> He's the person that you meet
> When you're picking at your feet,
> He's a person that you meet each day.

♦ *Kevin, at Baptist camp, Idaho, age ten, ca. 1978.*

Version Two:

> Oh the proctologist is a person in your neighborhood,
> In your neighborhood,
> In your neighborhood,
> Oh the proctologist is a person in your neighborhood,

He's the person that you pass
When you're picking at your ass,
He's a person that you meet each day.[12]

◆ *Kevin, at Baptist camp, Idaho, age ten, ca. 1978.*

(to the tune of "Rubber Ducky" from Sesame Street*)*

Sweaty Betty, you're my friend,
Sweaty Betty, you're the end,
Sweaty Betty, I'm awfully fond of you.
Sweaty Betty, joy of joys,
When I feel you, you make noise,
Sweaty Betty, you're my very best friend it's true.

Every day when I make my way to my beddy
I find my sweaty Betty there, hot and ready for me!
Rub a dub a dubbie ...

Sweaty Betty, you're the one
Who makes bedtime so much fun.
Sweaty Betty, I'm awfully fond of you.

◆ *John, Toledo, Ohio, ca. 1972-73.*[13]

SONGS WE ALL KNOW
—SLIGHTLY TWISTED

Nursery Rhymes

Part of America's shared culture is nursery rhymes. As a sign that one has outgrown the nursery, the verses below show that those reciting them have mastered adult concepts and language:[14]

Hickory dickory dock.
Two mice ran up the clock.
The clock struck one.
The other one escaped with only minor injuries.

◆ *Mitch, Long Island, in the early or mid 1970s.*[15]

Version One:

Mary had a little lamb
And put him on the heater.
Every time he turned around
He burned his little peter.

◆ *Daniel, Alaska, late 1970s.*

Version Two:

Mary had a little lamb.
She fed it castor oil.
And everywhere that Mary went,
It fertilized the soil.

◆ *Hank, Benham, Kentucky, 1958-59.*

Version Three:

Mary had a little lamb,
And the doctor fainted.

◆ *Hank, Benham, Kentucky, 1958-59.*[16]

Little Miss Muffet
Sat on a tuffet,
Eating her curds and whey.
Along came a spider
And sat down beside her

And said, "What's in the bowl, bitch?"

◆ *Hank, Benham, Kentucky, 1958-1959.*

Old Mother Hubbard
Went to the cupboard
To get her poor dog a bone,
But when she leaned over,
That old Rover drove her.
Rover had a bone of his own.

◆ *Hank, Loyall, Kentucky, 1961.*[17]

Peter, Peter, pumpkin eater,
Had a wife and couldn't keep her.
Put her in a pumpkin shell,
And there he beat her all to hell.

◆ *Daniel, Alaska, late 1970s.*

Twinkle, twinkle little star
Who the hell do you think you are,
Up in heaven you think you're it,
But down on Earth you're full of sh__.

◆ *Evelyn, Bronx, New York, ca. 1940s.*[18]

Patriotic Songs

Perhaps because many people find the national anthem of the United States unmelodic, there are many other patriotic songs that are sung almost as often as "The Star Spangled Banner." Parodies of such songs thus have a special sting:[19]

(to the tune of "God Bless America")

God bless my underwear,
My only pair.
Stand beside them and guide them
So they don't get a rip or a tear.
Through the washer, and the dryer,
From the dresser, back to me.
God bless my underwear,
My only pair.

◆ *Scott, Atlanta, Georgia, age nine, 1994, who learned it from a neighbor from California, age eight. A similar version comes from Janni Lee, Long Island, New York, ca. 1980.*[20]

"Over There" was a stirring song about going to fight in Europe in World War I. It was so effective, it won the song-writer a congressional medal in 1941:

(to the tune of "Over There")

Version One:

Underwear,
Underwear,
Get me a pair,
Buy me a pair,
Anywhere.

The whistle's blowing,
I've got to get going,
I'll get there yet,
If I have to get there bare.

Underwear,

Underwear.

♦ *Yvonne, camp in Michigan, late-1960s.*

Version Two:

Underwear!
Underwear!
Under there, we all wear
Underwear!

♦ *Lois, Ohio, ca. 1960s.*[21]

Below, two very different takes on "The Battle Hymn of the Republic." Version One is known as "The Skiing Song":

Version One:

The blood was on her bindings,
And her brains were on her skis.
Her intestines were hanging from
The highest of the trees.
They scraped her off the snow,
And they poured her in her boots,
And she ain't gonna ski no more.
Gory, gory, what a heck of a way to die.
Gory, gory, what a heck of a way to die.
Gory, gory, what a heck of a way to die.
And she ain't gonna ski no more.

♦ *Chandler, Bronx, New York, sung at Girl Scout meetings while waiting for the troop meetings to begin, ca. 1960.*

Version Two:

Oh, she wears her pink pajamas
In the summer, when it's hot,

And she wears her woolen undies
In the winter, when it's not,
And sometimes in the spring,
And sometimes in the fall,
She jumps between the sheets with nothing on at all!
Glory, glory for the springtime and the fall!
(repeat two times more)
When she jumps between the sheets with nothing on at all!

♦ *Sue, elementary school and junior high school in Brooklyn, New York, ca. 1967-75. "My older friend Hillary taught me this one."*[22]

"This Land is Your Land" was the "national anthem" of folksingers of the 1960s; the very sincerity of the song lends it to parody.

Version One:

(to the tune of "This Land Is Your Land")

This land is my land,
It isn't your land.
If you don't get off,
I'll shoot your head off.
I got a shotgun,
And you don't got one.
This land was made for only me.

♦ *Claire, Maryland, ca. 1960s. Also contributed by Sue, elementary school and junior high school in Brooklyn, New York, ca. 1967-75, and "Electro," New Jersey, ca. late 1970s.*

Version Two:

This land was your land,
But now it's my land.
I've got a shotgun

But you don't have one.
You tried to take it,
But you are naked.
This land was made for only me!

◆ *Judy, who learned it in 1980 from Jason in first grade, St. Peter's Lutheran Day School, Michigan. Also known to Claire, Silver Spring, Maryland, ca. 1963-1970.*

Version Three:

This land is my land,
It ain't your land.
I got a shotgun,
You ain't got one.
You better get off,
Or I'll blow your head off,
This land was made just for me.

As I was walking that ribbon highway,
I saw above me a hanging body.
I saw below me some blown-up guts.
This land was made just for me.

◆ *Katherine, Connecticut, age ten, 1993.*[23]

"Yankee Doodle" was itself a subversive rhyme, one intended by the British to mock the provincial Americans. Instead, the Revolutionary army turned it around and made it a song of pride. Now, it has become fit material for parody itself:

(to the tune of "Yankee Doodle")

Version One:

Yankee Doodle went to town
A-riding on a turtle,
Went into the ladies' room

And came out with a girdle.

◆ *Claire, Silver Spring, Maryland, mid-1960s.*

Version Two:

Yankee Doodle went to town
Riding on a gopher,
Bumped into a garbage can
And this is what fell over.

◆ *Jordy, Mamaroneck, New York, age eight, 1994.*[24]

Folk Songs

With the advent of widespread cheap recording technologies, the usage of the term "folk music" has gradually changed from meaning music transmitted orally from person to person to a marketing classification for "ethnic" music played on non-electrified instruments. The songs parodied below, however, are of the sort generally classified as "traditional" and thought of as wholesome by teachers.

(to the tune of "My Bonnie Lies Over the Ocean")

My bonny lay over the gas tank.
The contents she wanted to see.
I lighted a match to assist her.
Oh, bring back my Bonny to me!

◆ *Kevin, at Baptist camp, Idaho, age ten, ca. 1978.*[25]

(to the tune of "The Irish Washerwoman")

Oh, McTavish is dead and his brother don't know it.

His brother is dead and McTavish don't know it.
They're both lying dead in the very same bed,
And neither one knows that the other is dead!

♦ *Sue, elementary school and junior high school in Brooklyn, New York, ca. 1967-75.*[26]

(to the tune of "The Old Grey Mare")

The old grey mare, she went to the country fair,
Sat in a 'lectric chair,
Burned off her underwear.
The old grey mare, she ain't what she used to be
Many long years ago.

The old grey mare, she rode in a motor boat,
Blew off her petticoat.
(remaining lines missing)

♦ *Adrienne, Montana, learned between ages five and twelve, 1954 to 1960.*[27]

(to the tune of "Row, Row, Row Your Boat")

Roll, roll, roll the joint,
Pass it down the line,
Take a toke and hold your smoke
And blow your f___ing mind!

♦ *Sue, elementary school and junior high school in Brooklyn, New York, ca. 1967-75.*[28]

Legal drugs receive their share of attention from children also. Among liquors, tequila has a special place in popular culture, to the point of being featured in several rock songs, perhaps because of the myths associated with the worm at the bottom of the bottle.

(to the tune of "Havah Nagila")

Have a tequila,
Have a tequila,
Have a tequila,
It's good for you.

Have a tequila,
Have a tequila,
Have a tequila,
It's good for you.

Have one and run, run now,
Have one and run, run now,
Have one and run, run now,
To the liquor store. (HEY!)

Have one and run, run now,
Have one and run, run now,
Have one and run, run now,
To the liquor store.

And then, when you get there,
Go and buy a pint of whiskey.
Drink it up till you feel frisky.
Then you know you'll have to piss-ky,
And you hope you do not miss-ky.
Then you stop ... at the top ...
And do it one more time again!

Have a tequila,
Have a tequila,
Have a tequila,
It's good for you.

Have a tequila,
Have a tequila,

Have a tequila,
It's good for you!

◆ *Lynn, Willingboro, New Jersey, ca. mid-1960s.*[29]

We collected several take-offs on a very short Hebrew folk song:

Version One:

David, melech Yisroel,
Chai, chai, pizza pie ...

◆ *Bruce, Long Island, 1970s.*

Version Two:

Watermelon, ginger ale,
French fries, pizza-pie.

◆ *"Electro," New Jersey, ca. late 1970s.*

Version Three:

Coca Cola, ginger ale,
Hi-fi, pizza pie.

◆ *Claire, New York state, learned at camp in the late 1960s. Also, Jonathan and Sue, elementary school and junior high school in Brooklyn, New York, ca. 1967-75.*[30]

Pop Tunes

We discovered relatively few takeoffs on popular tunes, perhaps because popular artists have yet to become authority figures and hence figures of fun. But in the 1970s a wave of nostalgia for the 1950s swept over the country, which probably explains why a song was parodied twenty years after it was first recorded:

(to the tune of "Rock Around the Clock")

> When it's Saturday night, and you don't have a date,
> You can always stay home and masturbate.
> We're going to beat around the sheets tonight—
> Gonna beat beat beat till we lose our sight—
> We're gonna beat our meat all around the sheets tonight.

◆ *John, Toledo, Ohio, ca. 1972-73. Informant notes that "this was the real 'fight song' of the wrestling team; "Sweaty Betty" (above) was more common among the tennis players."*[31]

The Beach Boys were more than just a group, they were the crest of a popular wavefront. Not everybody rode it:

(to the tune of "California Girls")

> The East Coast girls put makeup on
>   with a trowel and a broom,
> And the Southern girls with the way they think
>   are little brides in search of a groom.
> The Midwest farmer's daughters have IQ's of sixty-three,
> And St. Louis girls with the way they look,
>   can't give it away for free ...

◆ *John, late 1970s, Washington University.*[32]

The Beatles seem to be an exception to the general rule, perhaps because their influence was so great that they have become more than mere music-industry icons:

(to the tune of "Yesterday")

Suddenly,
I'm not half the man I used to be,
I just had a vasectomy ...

◆ *Adam, from Albert Leonard High School, Honesdale, Pennsylvania, ca. 1970s.*[33]

(to the tune of "Hey Jude")

Hey Jude,
I know you're nude.
Don't try to fake it,
I caught you naked ...

◆ *Adam, Albert Leonard High School, Honesdale, Pennsylvania, ca. 1970s.*[34]

This is a "folk song" of recent vintage, and the subject of much controversy when it was first recorded in the 1960s, especially because it appealed to children:

(to the tune of "Puff the Magic Dragon")

Puff the Jewish Dragon
Lived in Palestine
And frolicked in the morning mist on Manischewitz wine.
Little Rabbi Goldberg
Loved that dragon Puff
And fed him lox and Matzoh balls
And other Jewish stuff.

◆ *Mitch, Suffolk, Long Island, 1972.*[35]

SUPERHEROES

Living people and historical characters are the figures usually presented to children as examples of heroes. But many times it is odd fictional characters, with some flaw that makes them outsiders, that children actually look to for inspiration. Still, the admiration these characters receive also makes them vulnerable to being brought down by parody, just as true authority figures and heroes are:

(First Voice)
(Second Voice)

Tarzan,
    Tarzan,
Swinging on a rubber band,
    Swinging on a rubber band,
Tarzan,
    Tarzan,
fell into a frying pan,
    Fell into a frying pan,
[Spoken] Ohhh, that's hot!
Now Tarzan has a tan.
    Now Tarzan has a tan.
Jane,
    Jane,
Flying in her aeroplane,
    Flying in her aeroplane.
Jane,
    Jane,
Crashed into a freeway lane.
    Crashed into a freeway lane.
[Spoken] Ohhh, that hurts!
Now Jane has a pain,

Now Jane has a pain,
And Tarzan has a tan.
    And Tarzan has a tan.
Cheetah,
    Cheetah,
Dancing to the beat-ah.
    Dancing to the beat-ah.
Cheetah,
    Cheetah,
Got eaten by amoeba.
    Got eaten by amoeba.
(Spoken) Ohhh, that's gross!
Now Cheetah's an amoeba,
    Now Cheetah's an amoeba,
And Jane has a pain,
    And Jane has a pain,
And Tarzan has a tan,
    And Tarzan has a tan.
And this is the end,
    And this is the end.
I won't sing any more.

◆ *Katzi, Thetford, Vermont, age 9, recently returned from Girl Scout camp in 1992.*[36]

Version One:

Tarzan the Monkey Man,
Swinging on a rubber band.
Pop goes the rubber band, down goes the Monkey Man.

◆ *Jim, St. Patrick's Parochial School, Bedford, New York, early 1960s.*[37]

Version Two:

(chanted along to the rhythm of the Batman *TV theme song)*

Batman ... Swingin' on a rubberband, 'long came Superman, punched him in the garbage can. Batman!

◆ *Mitch, Brooklyn, middle-late 1960s.*[38]

The campy TV show about the famous comic-book super-hero Batman inspired a whole generation to make fun of him. Who is the Generation X-er who didn't sing along with the theme music chorus, "Nuh-nuh nuh-nuh nuh-nuh nuh-nuh—FATman!"?[39] But the lack of lyrics limits the amount of parody one can set to that tune. Instead, Batman gets mixed up with Christmas:

Version One:

Jingle Bells, Batman smells,
Robin laid an egg.
The Batmobile lost a wheel
And the Joker got away.

◆ *Daniel, Eagle, Alaska, ca. 1970s.*

Version Two:

Jingle bells, Batman smells,
Robin laid an egg.
The Batmobile lost a wheel,
And Alfred broke his leg.

◆ *"MoorHardi," Tallahassee, Florida, in third grade, ca. 1970.*

Version Three:

Jingle bells, Batman smells,

Robin laid an egg.
The Batmobile lost a wheel,
And Batgirl lost her leg.
Jingle bells, Batman smells,
Joker got away.
The Batmobile's lost four wheels,
Commissioner's eating hay.

◆ *Elizabeth, Kingston, Jamaica, 1972.*[40]

King Kong, the giant ape, is both a powerful figure and an antihero. But in the original movie featuring Kong, and ever since, the audience's sympathy is for the ape, torn from his natural habitat, taken to someplace confusing, and used by unscrupulous people. He became a traditional American underdog and a powerful symbol for generations. Which, as we have seen, is merely an invitation to parody:

Down at the jungle
Where the trees grow,
There sits King Kong
As huge as a bear.
Along comes a banana
And hits him on the nose,
And poor King Kong
Has a sticky face.

◆ *Alice, Park Hill School, North Little Rock, Arkansas, age approximately 8-10, 1993.*[41]

CHAPTER NINE

THE LIFE & DEATHS OF BARNEY

The Barney Phenomenon. The mighty marketing machine of America goes marching on, to the tune of millions of dollars in licensed products sold with the image of the singing purple dinosaur.[1] Who is Barney? What is his message?

Barney is the "star" of a children's television program, aired primarily on public television since 1988. The format is quite simple: Barney, a stuffed purple dinosaur, magically comes to life every afternoon in a day-care center. A person in a stylized, neotenous dinosaur suit leads children (live actors) through a series of songs, games, and dances, usually focusing on some theme: sharing, imagination, helping each other, and so on. The show starts with a song explaining Barney as a "dinosaur from our imagination," sung to the tune of "Yankee Doodle." The show always closes with a different song, sung to the tune of "This Old Man."

It is this song, rather than the "origin" opening song, that is so frequently parodied.[2] These are the words as sung on the show: "I love you, you love me, We're a happy family./ With a great big hug and a kiss from me to you,/ Won't you say you'll love me, too?/ I love you, you love me,/ We're best friends like friends should be./ With a great big hug/ and a kiss from me to you,/ Won't you say you love me, too?"

Harmless enough, one would think. Yet the show and Barney have sparked both the devotion of a vast audience of children and their grateful parents, as well as a huge backlash of virulent hatred from not just an academic audience of media critics, but a mass audience of parents and childless people who wouldn't conceivably watch the show.[3] Part of this backlash is certainly due to traditional impulses to parody: the desire to denigrate a figure of authority, for instance, and the urge to show up the hypocrisy of the lesson and the difference between what the lesson says and the way life really appears to children.[4] But the Barney backlash seems to be more involved and broader in scope than most parodies of cultural trends. Goods with the Barney icon affixed have saturated the marketplace, familiarizing the country with at least the image of Barney and perhaps engendering resentment among adults who have no interest in that intrusion into their lives.

Indeed, Barney's message of undifferentiated universal love as expressed in his sign-off song has also penetrated to the wider culture, reaching far beyond that of the toddler set who actually watch the show. In the process, Barney has become a symbol for the whole idea of political correctness, and the parodies below can be seen as a grass-roots resistance to the extremes of that ideology. While adults ostensibly make fun of the show because it is aimed at the very young (ages three to six) and is simple in approach and subject matter and therefore not terribly interesting to them, in fact their parodies attack the idea of the "happy" non-nuclear family by substituting "dysfunctional" in the first verse.

The folk rhymes collected from children reveal perhaps a deeper reaction to the occasional ham-handed, politically correct preaching inserted amidst the simplified folk and pop tunes, the dances, and the games that form the bulk of the show's contents. Children, after all, are the targets for these messages. The contrast between the oversimplified mutual affection in the Barney song and the specific nature of the deaths awaiting the Purple One are striking. Children know life isn't that simple; death, though is a concrete fact, and it wears a million faces:

Sherman & Weisskopf

How Do We Hate Thee?
Let Us Count the Ways:

VARIANTS ON HOW BARNEY DIES

Version One:

I hate you,
You hate me,
Let's get together and kill Barney
With a nine millimeter and shoot him in his head,
Aren't you glad that Barney's dead?

◆ *Alexis, Bronx, New York, age eleven, 1994: She explains that this is to tease younger kids who like Barney, who then leap to defend him by pummeling the versifier.*

Version Two:

I hate you,
You love me,
I ran Barney up the street
With a nine-nine millimeter to his head.
Pow! Pow! Pow! Now Barney's dead.

◆ *Decarlo, North Little Rock, Arkansas, age eleven, 1993.*

Version Three:

I hate you,
You hate me,
Let's group up and kill Barney
With an 8-16 shoot him in the head.
Hurray, Hurray, Barney's dead.

◆ *Joanna, Montreal, Quebec, age eight, 1994.*

Version Four:

I hate you,
You hate me,
Together we can kill Barney
With a knife in his stomach and a bullet in his head.
Aren't you glad that Barney's dead?

◆ *Myekia, North Little Rock, Arkansas, between ages 8 and 12, 1993.*

Version Five:

I hate you,
you hate me,
I threw Barney—I keep Barney up a tree—
With a knife in his stomach and a bullet in his head.
Aren't you glad that Barney's dead?

◆ *Brenda, North Little Rock, Arkansas, sixth grade, 1994.*

Version Six:

I hate you, you hate me,
We put Barney in a tree.
Pull the trigger,
Hit him in the head.
Whoopsy daisy Barney's dead!

◆ *Alex, Westchester, New York, age six, 1993.*

Version Seven:

I hate you, you hate me,
I got a machine gun
To kill Barney.
One big shot,
Barney's on the floor,

No more purple dinosaur.

◆ *Alex, Westchester, New York, age six, 1993.*

Version Eight:

I like you, you like me,
Let's get together and kill Barney,
With a great big shot gun,
We'll blow off Barney's head.
Whoops, I think that Barney's dead.

◆ *Jennie, Northern New Jersey, approximately. age nine, 1994.*

Version Nine:

I hate you, you hate me,
Let's get together and kill Barney,
With a shotgun blast and Barney's on the floor.
No more purple dinosaur.

◆ *Unidentified eleven year old from New Hampshire, 1994; a similar version was collected from an unidentified girl from Park Hill Elementary North Little Rock, Arkansas between eight and twelve years of age, 1994.*

Version Ten:

I hate you,
You hate me,
Let's get together and kill Barney,
With a great big knife and a shot from me to you.
Thank god Barney is dead, yaahoo!

◆ *Andrew, West Paterson, New Jersey, age eight, 1994.*

A quite different variant from the same informant:

Version Twelve:

I hate you,
You hate me,
Barney shot me in the knee,
So I shot him in back and he fell to the floor.
No more purple dinosaur.

◆ *Andrew, West Paterson, New Jersey, age eight, 1994.*

Version Thirteen:

I hate you,
You hate me,
Let's kick Barney out of TV
With a kick from me to you.
Let's kick Barney ....
(Rest of verse is garbled).

◆ *Matthew (informant Andrew's brother), West Paterson, New Jersey, age five, 1994.[5]*

Not all of the parodies of Barney's song involve killing Barney. Some directly contradict the message of familial happiness, but in a far more graphic way than adult parodies:[6]

I hate you, you hate me,
We a ... family
With a punch in the face and a kick from me to you.
Won't you say you hate me too?

◆ *Girl from Park Hill Elementary North Little Rock, Arkansas, between eight and twelve years of age, 1994.[7]*

We did collect one parody of Barney's opening tune:

Section Three: The Commercial World

(to the tune of "Yankee Doodle")

Barney is a dinosaur,
He comes from outer space.
He kills everybody
By farting in their face.

◆ *Michelle, Bronx, New York, 6 years old, 1994.*[8]

BARNEY AND THE PINK TRIANGLE

The height of the AIDS panic predated Barney by a few years, but the public awareness programs and education about "safe sex" were in full swing as Barney mania hit. Barney is a sensitive, nurturing sort, not a particularly macho character, and thus may be vulnerable to being labeled homosexual. Also, an earlier rhyme about lesbians used the the same opening line ("I love you, you love me"). All of which perhaps led to the following graphic parody, submitted by the father of one of several "sixth grade girls who want to keep their identities hidden (for reasons which will soon become apparent)":

I love you, you love me,
Barney has got H.I.V.
Barney jumped on Baby Bop one time.
That's called rape and that's a crime.

I hate you, you hate me,
Barney died of H.I.V.
Tripped on a skate and fell on a whore,
No more purple dinosaur.

I hate you, you hate me,
Baby Bop f___ed with Barney.

He gave a hop and she said to stop,
Now they have to see the Doc.

◆ *Informants, sixth grade girls, New Hampshire, 1994. The father notes: "It seems that AIDS awareness training does work."*[9]

Not all the songs doing violence to Barney are parodies of his own song. This one, collected by author Weisskopf while standing in line at the bank, is sung to the tune of the Christmas carol "Joy to the World:"

Joy to the world,
Barney's dead.
They bar-be-qued his head.

Don't worry 'bout Barney,
They flushed him down the potty,
And 'round and 'round he goes,
And 'round and 'round he goes.
Barney's dead.

◆ *Informants: Two sisters, approximately seven and ten, singing it to their toddler brother, overheard by author Weisskopf in Riverdale, New York in 1993. The two girls did a circular dance around their brother's carriage. When enjoined by their mother to stop singing because it was upsetting their brother, who liked Barney, they replied indignantly that the song was about Barney.*[10]

Barney has taken on the character of such entertainment icons as Charlie Chaplin and Batman and, like them, made his way into other subversive rhymes unrelated to the original parodies of his own show. This is a hand-clapping chant:

Tic tac toe,
Three in a row.

Barney got shot by a G.I. Joe.
Went to the doctor and the doctor said:
"Whump! Barnie's dead.
Shot in the head."
Be he live
Or be he dead,
We'll grind his bones
To make us bread.
One. Two. Three.

◆ *Reyla, Ontario, Canada, age thirteen, 1994, who learned it in first grade (1988).*[11]

NOTES

Full bibliographic information on the books and authors cited in the notes can be found in the bibliography beginning on page 249.

INTRODUCTION

1. There are many books available on the subject of adult rituals of deliberate chaos, from Sir James G. Frazier's *The Golden Bough,* available in many editions, which, although dated, gives a good overview, to author Sherman's *A Sampler of Jewish-American Folklore,* which includes a discussion of Purim and the happy drunkenness that may accompany it.

2. Issac Asimov, a raconteur and lifetime student of the dirty joke, has noted that "a joke is nothing in itself; it must be told. A joke is a social phenomena; an interaction among people ... it breaks down reserve, eases tension, establishes contact. But to be told effectively, a joke must be told well, and talents in that respect vary." (Isaac Asimov's *Treasury of Humor: A Lifetime Collection of Favorite Jokes, Anecdotes, and Limericks with Copious Notes on How to Tell Them and Why.*)

3. Dr. Geneva Smitherman in her introduction to Double Snaps notes that the older rhyming style of the dozens is not so prevalent as it once was. But perhaps the subversive folk form snapping may be losing its rhymes because of its adoption by older people, such as the comedians and radio personalities who wrote snaps specifically for the two collections of snaps Dr. Smitherman discusses. (Snaps, and its sequel, Double Snaps are edited by James Percelay et al.)

4. For clarity, punctuation and spelling has been regularized.

SECTION ONE

CHAPTER ONE

1. As Gershon Legman documents in his monumental study of the dirty joke, *Rationale of the Dirty Joke,* the recitation of truly offensive jokes

takes on a "topping" aspect, with each participant seeking to tell a joke dirtier than the last. (Legman quotes Nietzsche on sick jokes, and talks about the role of audience participation: "the audience has partaken guiltily with him." But rather than merely serving a psychological function, the sharing of subversive verse serves an important anthropological and social one: defining the "us" in contrast to the "them" one is not supposed to say it in front of—the teller fully knowing that if caught, teller and listener are both punished for their knowledge and participation.) The competitive aspect found in urban practice of bandying quick insults, called "snapping" or "ranking" (*Snaps*, op. cit.) has a similar competitive aspect. As with both of these other forms of transmitting folklore orally, the transmission of the subversive verse, especially the pure grossout, usually involves one-upmanship.

2.   When we set about putting this book together, this rhyme was the one most frequently recognized by children and adults alike, and the one most likely to be quoted in one form or another. Variants of it could fill a book in itself; the rhyme has become so widespread across North America that there is no one "correct" version and the origin is impossible to trace. "Gopher Guts" tends to bring about a good deal of arguments both among children and adults about the proper ghastly ingredients, the one constant remaining those gopher guts themselves. Nor is each individual rhyme above alteration: one informant, Jeanne, reported a version from ca. 1972, Pitman, New Jersey, that ended in "And that's what I had for lunch/ But I forgot my spoon." She then added that a couple of years later her version collected a final line, "But I've got a straw."

Versions One through Four exist simply to revolt; they also add the frustration of not having a spoon with which to partake of this "feast." Version Five adds an unexpected touch of stardom, bringing in Elvis Presley. The introduction of celebrities into children's folk rhymes is a very common occurrence; see, for example, Charlie Chaplin's appearances in the rhymes in Chapter Two and the various appearances of other famous figures in Chapter Eight. Version Six introduces the specifically Southern element of barbecue, one notably missing from Northern versions. Version Ten adds a parody of an anxious mother trying to coax her child to eat. The informant, a folklorist's dream, has added a fascinating and annotated list of local ingredients. Version Eleven turns the mother's anxious words into an insult by adding a specific child's name. Version Twelve not only introduces a new element—not merely porpoise pus, but prehistoric porpoise pus, a beautifully revolting tongue twister—it includes the smug implication, "And you ate it without knowing what you ate," guaranteed to further disgust the listener. Version Thirteen, one of the most recent we collected, turns violent, with a group of crazy people fighting over those guts. The standard "greasy grimy" has been transformed by the folk process into a Spoonerized version. Versions

Fourteen through Eighteen turn the rhyme into an insult song. Version Nineteen is unusual in that it consists of a combination of two folk rhymes. "The Bedbugs and the Cooties" usually is attached to a sociopolitical statement about being arrested, or sometimes about being falsely arrested. (See Chapter Six for more variants.) Version Twenty seems to be a good place to stop, as it is a warning to stay away from such dangerous things as gopher guts!

Other folklorists have, not surprisingly, collected their own variants on the gopher-gut theme. See, for instance, those collected in the 1970s from Delaware and Utah recorded in Simon Bronner's *American Children's Folklore* and those collected in the same decade from Vermont in Scott E. Hastings, Jr.'s *Miss Mary Mac All Dressed in Black*.

3. This is a very popular rhyme across North America. Although worms are edible (just as Version Four claims!) and are apparently a good source of protein to boot—there have even been recipes that call for worms as an ingredient—the concept of eating the creatures remains disgusting to most children and adults alike. The idea has given rise to such books as *How to Eat Fried Worms* by Thomas Rockwell, in which a boy agrees to eat a worm a day for fifteen days in order to win a bet. Partial versions were also contributed by John in Alabama, Lois in Ohio, Judy in Connecticut, and Mark in California. Though ubiquitous, this rhyme was usually recalled only in fragments.

    See also the version collected in the 1970s from Vermont by Scott E. Hastings, Jr. in his *Miss Mary Mac All Dressed in Black*. Mary and Herbert Knapp cite another version, possibly from their own recollections (no specific data is given) in *One Potato, Two Potato*.

    Folklore, like anything else, changes with the time. This rhyme shows how a parody survives the actual song. While "Reuben, Reuben, (I've been thinking)" is no longer a popular song—although the melody is still relatively familiar and has been used in commercials—this gross-out parody remains quite popular among children in North America. As with the eating worms verses, this is not only a gross-out, but also a parody of the mother's traditional nag not to touch or ingest dangerous substances. The difference is that while eating a worm won't kill you, ingesting turpentine will—and these rhymes humorously underline that lesson. A similar version collected in 1949 from Cherrydale, Virginia, is recorded in Francelia Butler's *Skipping Around the World* and in *Miss Mary Mack and Other Children's Street Rhymes* compiled by Cole, Joanna and Stephanie Calmenson. Peter and Iona Opies, in *I Saw Esau*, record three rhymes about Julius Caesar, at least one of which fits the scansion and pattern of "Lincoln, Lincoln." They also record a rhyme from their own childhoods in which the word "queen" is repeated in the first line that seems to fit the pattern. This one is about Queen Caroline (George IV's wife) who washes her hair in turpentine to make it shine.

4. There are enough childhood parodies of nursery rhymes to fill a book in themselves! A good many of them start out in perfectly normal fashion, then conclude with a "zinger." Some variants of "Little Miss Muffet" end not with her eating the spider, but merely in the spider asking, "What's new, broad?" or similar slangy greetings. See Chapter Eight for an example of this.

5. For more on the adventures of bedbugs, see the combination version of the bedbugs' baseball game and "Greasy Grimy Gopher Guts" earlier in this chapter, and the more complete versions of the bedbugs' baseball game in Chapter Six.

6. This is another song parody that can be dated with a fair amount of accuracy: "I'm Looking Over a Four-Leafed Clover" was written by Mort Dixon and Harry Woods in 1927. The reference to "Cocoa Puff train" in Version Two further dates that version to the 1960s, when Cocoa Puffs cereal was advertised on television with that train. A 1970s version of this gross-out rhyme called "My Dead Dog Rover" was recorded by the group Hank, Stu, Dave and Hank and was a "hit" on the "Dr. Demento" syndicated radio show.

7. These are fairly common rhymes in North America, and have been for at least a century. They are particularly fun for the very young because the subject matter isn't all that threatening and the end leads naturally to the onomatopoeic euphony of "eeuw." Francelia Butler cites a version of "Peanut" collected in Elyria, Ohio in 1930, while a similar "Ooey-Gooey" version, spelled "Euey Guey," was collected in Vermont in the early 1970s and was included by Scott Hastings, Jr. in his *Miss Mary Mac All Dressed in Black*.

8. Grandmothers turn up as figures in children's parodies a fair number of times. Why this should be is yet another subject for Freudians to ponder. For more examples of grandmothers turning up in unlikely places, see Chapter Four and Chapter Eight. Mary and Herbert Knapp report a similar version, unfortunately without citing sources, in their *One Potato, Two Potato* .

9. Dirty clothes, or more specifically, clothes that go unwashed for far too long, are a fairly rare subject for children's parodies, although one rather common for parental complaints! Underwear, however, is a very popular subject in children's rhymes. See, for example, rhymes in Chapters Four and Eight.

CHAPTER TWO

1. This rhyme will delight Freudians, with its symbolic snake and implied wound/sexual encounter. It's a common jump rope rhyme both in the

United States and abroad. Francelia Butler, in *Skipping Around the World*, has collected similar versions, dating from the 1970s and 1980s, from Canterbury, England, Yukon Territory, Canada, and the Virgin Islands. Although the color of Cinderella's dress is different in each of her variants, all save that recorded in the Virgin Islands featured the mistake of kissing the snake. As one Little Rock girl stated to author Sherman about the basic form of the rhyme, it "is just something that everybody says." Cinderella's name has been separated from her story and incorporated into children's folk rhymes in this country for well over a hundred years. Since her story is one of the most popular folktales in the world—almost six hundred variants have been collected by folklorists—and is almost always among the first that children hear from parents or teachers, it's not surprising that her name has stuck in their memories. Although this particular rhyme invariably features Cinderella, other, unrelated rhymes reveal similarly casual insertions of names of popular fictional characters such as Santa Claus, Batman, and Barney, as well as actual people such as Charlie Chaplin and the ubiquitous Elvis Presley.

These two rhymes are an example of the folk process in action. While the more common forms of the Cinderella rhyme involve that deliciously shuddery (and symbolic) act of kissing a snake, the transmission of folklore sometimes resembles a game of Telephone, in which bits of information are lost or changed along the way. In these two versions, the rhythm of the counting rhyme outweighs the importance of the actual words, which need only keep the beat. Cinderella also takes front stage in several jump rope rhymes and counting games in which the sexual content has been almost totally lost in the transmission from one child to another:

Version One:

Cinderella dressed in lace
Went upstairs to powder her face
How many puffs did it take? (counts)

Version Two:

Cinderella dressed in red
Went upstairs to bake some bread
How many loaves did she make? (counts)

♦ *Bailey, age unspecified but between nine and eleven, Park Hill Elementary School, North Little Rock, Arkansas, 1994.*

2. Version One is a very new variation on an older rhyme, showing how folklore mutates over the years. The first part of the rhyme, up to "the

meadow's in the park," is a modern version of a joke-lore rhyme that's been wandering the United States for the last hundred years or so. It can be fairly accurately dated thanks to the reference to a steamboat and a telephone; Robert Fulton's invention first appeared commercially in 1806, while the telephone first appeared in 1876. However, the second part of the rhyme, beginning with "D-A-R-K," is very new. Neither Mary and Herbert Knapp, in their *One Potato, Two Potato*, nor Simon J. Bronner, in *American Children's Folklore* record it, while the version collected by Scott E. Hastings, Jr. in his book of New England children's lore, *Miss Mary Mac All Dressed in Black*, includes a partial version that stops short of "I know I know my mother ..." The reference to the 18 hour bra, a Playtex brand—also mentioned in a similar version from Mischel, an eight-year-old girl from Mamaroneck, New York—further dates that portion of the rhyme to within the last twenty years. An almost identical version from Anne, a ten year old from New Jersey, added an unexpected touch of modern school math by changing the "18 hour bra" to "I know I know my sister with the 18 meter bra." Another almost identical version from Katherine, an eleven year old from New Hampshire, changed Lulu to Susie but included that "18 meter bra." Yet another almost identical version from "MoorHardi," ca. 1972, Louisville, Kentucky, corroborates the hypothesis that while the first part of the rhyme tends to be transmitted virtually unchanged, the ending is in a constant state of flux. "MoorHardi's" version eliminated the "D-A-R-K" segment, but ended with a play on words: "The cows are in the pasture/ Making chocolate pies," which is similar to Version Five from Alabama in the early '70s.

Such tricky rhymes as "Miss Lucy," which never quite become actively "dirty," were often memorized in the nineteenth century and recited before company as set pieces! But this form of almost-dirty rhyme is much older than the U.S. The Elizabethans were singing such bawdy, almost-dirty songs in Shakespeare's time (see, for example, "Here Dwells a Pretty Maid," a catch attributed to William Cranford, 1650-1675[?] and recorded in *The Art of the Bawdy Song*, The Baltimore Consort, Dorian Recordings, 1992), as were other folk before them.

Why is this type of rhyme so popular? Possibly because it's a particularly satisfying form of wordplay, involving anticipation and clever twists, flirting with taboos but never overtly breaking them. And it has an added attraction for children: when caught by adults, those children can say in feigned innocence, "We were just singing a song ..."

Despite some slight variations in the words, the rhyme is always chanted rather than sung. Christina, a young teen from Arizona, knows "Lulu" as the chant for a hand clapping game, as do several younger children, but "Lulu" has also appeared in jump rope games as well.

A note on Jessica's variant: While the content of the rhyme is essentially unchanged, in this very modern rendering the political climate has turned "Miss Lucy" into "Ms." Version Two shows that other versions of this rhyme star other women. However, Helen and her tugboat seem to be unique; her name appears, as far as we could tell, only in this version, as does the tugboat. Notice the milder comment to the operator, mimicking adult conversations, to simply return the dime if the phone call isn't completed. The conclusive ending, in which the rhyme becomes Helen's last words, is unique to this informant, although not to children's folklore. The many possible names of the rhyme's protagonist can lead into some odd arguments. The following "dialogue" is taken almost verbatim from a computer bulletin board discussion: "I remember Lulu ... only we called her Mary. Same basic lyrics, though."—Kathy, New Jersey. "We called her Lulu in Ohio."—Susan, now from New York, originally from Ohio. "And all those words about Lulu were part of the song about Rosie that I couldn't remember all the words to."—Janni, St. Louis. "Sally had a steamboat. Sally. Sally."—Michael, no location given. The last line in the "conversation" sums up the usual reaction of adults to folkloric proddings: "Thanks for remembering Lulu. Chanted right along with it once you knocked the cogs loose for me."—Eric, no location given.

3. This incomplete version of the "Miss Lucy" rhyme includes an unexpected switch into "Skip to My Lou" and out again! This is typical of the folk process: just as in those cases in which bits of stories or songs disappear during transmission, so unconnected story or song elements crop up and merge unexpectedly, often through a lapse of memory on the part of the reciter. When this insertion is successful, it remains. Cindy, a storyteller and children's librarian from the Boston area, drew a blank during the telling of the traditional scary story, "The Golden Arm," and hastily invented a new element. At a later date, she overheard a boy, not one who had been in the original session, recite "her" variant, which he had learned from other children. "Her" variant had entered the folk tradition!

4. This is perhaps the most unusual variant we collected, since it is the only one featuring a male protagonist. Johnny shows a stereotypical "male" temper, stopping the bell by blasting it with dynamite, while the reference to the Iron Curtain dates it clearly to the Cold War era.

5. Here we have a new heroine, one who has an almost risque reputation. Notice, for instance, the words "what she once learned in France." In this country, France has always had a reputation for things romantic and/or erotic; in the Victorian era in particular, erotic books and paintings often were imported from France—and people still "French kiss." Suzanne's song, "Off the Mandalay Shore," probably dates this rhyme to the Victorian era as well. A similar version is recorded by Jerry Silverman in *The Dirty Song Book*.

6.   For more on Tiny Tim, see Chapter Three.

7.   This rhyme begins with a well-known couplet, then turns into something very different indeed! The archaic "maiden" has probably crept in from some other source, since the rest of the rhyme is down to earth, including the final couplet with the sudden insertion of that "taboo" word. Gophers, native to America, crop up again and again in children's folklore, sometimes as instigators of trouble, as in this rhyme, sometimes as victims providing the traditional greasy, grimy guts, though why they appear remains a matter for speculation. One theory, proposed by writer Constance Ash, is that these folkloric gophers are reflections of the days when children—boys in particular—used to be offered bounties to kill gophers. It is interesting to note that the price for a "cocktail ginger ale" hasn't changed from 1959 to the early 1970s. The later version from the Bronx ends on a distinctly aggressive note, however.

8.   This sort of deceptive song, which starts out almost cloyingly sweet then ends with a zinger, was popular in the last century. They were probably inspired by a song in vogue at the time, and are still being sung by children today—usually when adults aren't listening. A comment from one informant, Creede, who also provided a partial version: "A friend of mine and I used to love to sing it when we were kids; it always sounded suggestive enough to tickle a fourteen year old's fancy." A similar version under the title "There Was an Old Farmer" is found in Silverman's *The Dirty Song Book*.

9.   Like the "Lulu" rhyme, this one also avoids outright profanity, though it makes no bones about what Rosie's been doing! Rosie would be "going away" to have her baby to spare her family shame; it was not uncommon in the days before legalized abortion for a girl who had "gotten herself in the family way" to be sent away, ostensibly to visit relatives.

10.   This is more or less a "sequel" to Version One of "Ms./Miss Lucy," showing the outcome of Rosie's "going away" and returning. The idea of putting a baby in a toilet is, of course, horrifying to adults but deliciously vicious to children, particularly with the unvoiced implication of flushing away an unwanted younger sibling (or, for that matter, an unwanted offspring). The mention of the toilet also reflects warning from parents to play away from it, itself a fascinating object on many levels, from technical to psychological.

11.   Here the horrifying image of the baby in the toilet has been transferred to the more innocuous one of the baby in the tub. It ends with the mildly "taboo" but satisfying (spoken) burp. The by-now traditional name of Tim has been turned here into "Tiny Tim," almost certainly after the Charles Dickens character, not the TV "star" of the late 1960s and '70s! And Rosie/LueLue has become Miss Suzy.

12. Here new elements enter the rhyme, which in Arizona is used as part of a hand-clapping game though children in other areas reported it as a jump rope rhyme. The idea of the monster child or being who attempts to eat everything and everyone in sight is a very ancient one and quite common in world folklore, turning up in tales everywhere from England to Asia. Scott Hastings, Jr. collected an even more "violent" version in his *Miss Mary Mac All Dressed in Black* in which the monster baby goes on to eat the doctor et al. until he burps them all back up again. A good example of this widespread folkloric theme of the monster baby or being can be found in "The Clayman and the Golden Stag," a Saami tale collected by James Riordan in *The Sun Maiden and the Crescent Moon: Siberian Folk Tales.* As for the lady with the alligator purse, this is a detail folklorists love, since it helps date the age of this variant to prior to the 1970s, when such purses ceased being fashionable.

13. Rosie/LueLue/Miss Suzy has changed names yet again, this time to Molly. Here the bathtub element disappears completely except for the soap, and the baby becomes a relatively innocuous teddy bear. Note, however, that in this variant, the bear eats the soap and dies. One can try to euphemize, but the nastiness will sneak in!

14. This and similar non-graphic folk rhymes are often used to poke relatively gentle fun at budding romances. They are frequently inserted into jump rope games, much to the embarrassment of the couple and the delight of the chanters. It's interesting to notice that in our modern version, it is the man who pushes the baby carriage. But in Cole and Calmenson's *Miss Mary Mack*, which contains "street verse" collected by the authors and their friends and packaged for children, it is again the girl who pushes the carriage.

15. This is an even more innocuous version than Version One. Although it still could be used to make fun of two lovers, it doesn't specifically call them by name. Nor is anyone actually pushing that baby carriage with its twin cargo. This rhyme's trip from Maine to Alaska shows just how far a good rhyme can travel!

16. This time the song returns to name-specific parody, both of the couple kissing and of the unfortunate classmate who has been transformed into a very non-idealized baby. One of the most popular taunts of one child to another is that he or she is nothing but a big baby! The "naked hula dance," which is an odd addition to the inventory of normal baby activities, is a transfer from another category of folk rhyme.

17. Here a new line has been added to the basic rhyme: "Then comes the baby drinking alcohol." Although children have been faced with stern warnings at home, on television and in school about the dangers involved in drinking, the six-year-old informant almost certainly had no idea of the significance of this line, but had added it simply to fit the rhyme. Seven

year old Lorelei's version, with that energetic baby, certain strikes a chord with weary parents!

18. This is the only example we have of this verse—it may be a new one in the making!

19. The basic rhyme is a fairly old one in this country, including the hint of an illicit birth in "call the judge," but such specific elements as "send it down the elevator" show that it has become an urban, twentieth century rhyme, with the implication of casual violence in getting rid of an unwanted birth. A jump-rope, counting version mentioning sending the baby "up the elevator" can be found in *Anna Banana: One Hundred and One Jump-Rope Rhymes* compiled by Joanna Cole.

20. This song is in its way as basic as the many "I sat me down beside a thorn" folksongs—those in which a sadder but wiser woman bewails her "fallen" state—that are so popular around the world. It parallels the folksong warnings rather remarkably, considering that the informants were children almost certainly not well-acquainted with the original songs.

21. Obviously, this parody/warning dates from after the opening of *My Fair Lady* on Broadway in the mid-1950s! A skit in *Laugh-In*, the television show of the 1960s and 1970s, featured a "pregnant" Ruth Buzzi singing a more euphemized version. Author Sherman also incompletely remembers a variant that almost certainly dates from before the *Laugh-In* episode, as does Diane, location unknown, who remembers, "We did this [parody] about a month before Buzzi did—and were so proud of ourselves when the same (approximately) thing was on TV." Author Sherman also remembers seeing a humorous greeting card fairly recently featuring a very pregnant woman lamenting, "I should have danced all night!"

22. This is one of many similar parodies using this melody. Although this version ends with pregnancy, others end with the actual birth. One rhyme collected in the United States in 1974 by Francelia Butler in *Skipping Around the World* ends with the lines, "My father jumped for joy/ to see a baby boy."

23. We also ran across another variant that featured "Horace" and baby "Doris." The tune it uses is the theme from the movie *The Bridge Over the River Kwai*, and was also utilized by Comet in an ad campaign. For more parodies of this tune, see Chapters Six and Seven.

24. This is a truly nasty insult rhyme, implying not only that the indicated victim is willing to do "blow jobs" for hire, but that he will do them for ridiculously low pay. It also gets in a jibe at unionism as well. For more insult rhymes without the graphic sexual angle, see Chapter Four.

25. This youthful strip-tease is probably done only by girls who have a high amount of self-confidence—and an early awareness of their power over the opposite sex. It is, of course, never performed where there is any

chance of being seen by an adult.

26. The use of the word "fairy" to denote a homosexual has been gradually slipping out of favor in the United States; many articles have been written about why homosexuals were compared to folkloric beings in the first place, though the connection may be that the fairy folk were often described as being wildly sexual in ways outside the "accepted norm." Regarding green, this is a traditional folkloric fairy color that has been transferred over in modern folklore to the preferred color of homosexuals, particularly those looking for others. Lee, an informant from Massachusetts, noted that in the 1960s "it was specifically green socks on Thursday that allegedly branded the male wearer as homosexual," while author Sherman recalls a belief from the 1970s that wearing *any* green clothing on a Thursday meant the wearer was homosexual. Similar anti-green prejudices have been recorded from several informants. It says a good deal about the strength of homophobia in the United States that the thought of wearing a "forbidden" color should arouse genuine alarm.

27. This version dates from approximately the same era, in which Elvis Presley was already a cult figure; the idea that any girl could possibly not like him was enough, at least in this rhyme, to brand that girl as a "lesie," or lesbian. Notice that in this verse and in the previous one—as in many similar variants, such as that collected by Mary and Herbert Knapp in *One Potato, Two Potato*—the accusation of being homosexual is aimed primarily at girls, although gender uncertainties and insecurities are equally as common in boys. See Note 28 of this chapter for a less biased rhyme.

28. These two rhymes, in their current form, are definitely off-shoots of the "Let's Kill Barney" songs, all of which are parodies of Barney's "I Love You, You Love Me," which of course is, in turn, based on the well-known children's folksong, "This Old Man." However, we have also collected an older, pre-Barney version with words identical to Version One but meant to be sung to the tune of "Little Brown Jug." Informants who knew this version included Nancy, ca. 1973, Washington, D.C., Meg, ca. 1975, Wisconsin, and Elizabeth, ca. 1977, Harristown, Pennsylvania. For more on anti-Barney rhymes, see Chapter Nine.

   Children's folk rhymes, like all folklore, stay basically the same even while constantly absorbing new elements. While children often reflect their parents or teachers' attitudes about sex, sex education, and sexual orientation, for better or for worse, their rhymes are beginning to show a new openness about and an understanding of (if not necessarily acceptance of) those different orientations. While the rhymes cited here are of recent origin, it's also unlikely that such relatively tolerant rhymes could have appeared before the gay rights movement of the last three decades brought the issue of sexual orientation so blatantly into the public eye. See, for example, the earlier rhymes cited in Notes 26 and 27 of this chapter. Interestingly enough, these two variants-on-a-theme were collected from two children in different parts of the country, New Hampshire and Wisconsin, who had never met. Folklore travels by many and mysterious ways!

29. This song, strictly speaking, isn't a children's folk rhyme, since it's been sung in various versions by adults as well, from the end of the nineteenth century to now—but children have definitely made it their own, and sing it in their own variants. The idea of a grass skirt falling down and showing all is a bit of slapstick over which children giggle. The idea of forbidden or embarrassing nudity is extended to cover underwear as well; there's a whole separate category of folklore dealing with such traditional worries as "patent leather shoes reflecting up" and thereby offering boys a tantalizing glimpse of a girl's panties. A very popular related taunt is often chanted by children to any of their group who is unfortunate enough to let underwear show: "I saw Spain (or London), I saw France, I saw (name's) underpants." —Jim, ca. 1960s, Westchester, New York, and Meg, ca. 1960s, Pewaukee, Wisconsin, among others. The concept of the hula dance as titillating shows up in folk rhymes where it doesn't really fit.

30. Why have those grass-skirt wearing girls travelled from Polynesia to France? Who can say! France is a very popular location for this type of rhyme; Francelia Butler cites two examples in *Skipping Around the World*, one from Virginia, in which Charlie Chaplin "went to France to teach the girlies how to dance," the other from Australia, in which Mr. Chaplin again appears to teach those ladies how to dance, only to have his pants begin to fall down. The variant quoted here, though, is different in that it also has its roots in the not-quite dirty type of song in which the risque word is never spoken.

31. And here Mr. Chaplin makes another appearance, again as a dance instructor. Although the last line seems to be nonsense, it is almost certainly a corrupted version of one collected by Francelia Butler from Cherrydale, Virginia in 1944, which concludes with the mildly risque "And touch the bottom of a submarine," at which point the reciting children, giggling, would touch their own backsides. A similar version to Butler's is found in *Miss Mary Mack* as a counting jump-rope game, except that Chaplin goes to "war" rather than a place to teach the ladies to dance. The verse is continued with dance instructions that are in fact square dance calls until the instruction to "turn your back on the submarine."

32. This pair of daring rhymes is unusual in that it shows both the "boys'" and "girls'" versions. Both include voyeurism and the titillating idea of secretly seeing the other gender naked. The "girls'" version is the more daring since it actually mentions that "taboo" word, penis.

33. Version Six of the voyeurism rhyme may have the genders confused at the end. Wouldn't the men be less interested in watching women wearing at least some clothing? This rhyme has quite a list of "who told whom," although it seems a little doubtful that it was actually repeated on television. See also Chapter One for a gross-out version.

34. This insult rhyme gets its sting from the implication of abnormally large genitals; it well might have been turned into a boasting rhyme by older boys! As is often the case in children's folklore, names of famous characters are brought into the rhyme, whether or not they fit. It's more often Tarzan who's seen swinging on a rubber band. For more on Tarzan, Superman, and King Kong, see Chapter Eight.

35. As the informant told this counting-out rhyme, she and the two boys with her stood in a circle facing each other. All three put their right feet forward, and she pointed at them in turn as she said each word. Tarzan takes more than his share of falls from vines, rubber bands, and the like in children's folklore. For more, see Chapter Eight.

36. This rhyme shows the folk process in action: The majority of variants don't have that unfortunate constipated soldier. Much more frequent is mention of "a Continental Soldier," which may possibly date this song to the Continental Army of the eighteenth century, or at least, along with "Turkey in the Straw," to 1834—and which phrase is easily misheard as "constipated" by a child. This song probably originated in the military; it has a definite marching cadence. There are also male and female versions of this song! Author Sherman: "I remember a version—though from where and when, I don't recall—that changed 'balls' to 'boobs.' It was, needless to say, sung only by girls." This song, like many folk rhymes deemed too frank, has been softened by adults. Bowdlerized versions can be found on *Barney and Friends* and in interactive children's books with the line, "Do your ears hang low?"

    We did encounter songs outside of the purview of this volume learned at a young age in the military or in college, including this variant collected by Erwin Strauss at M.I.T. in the early sixties. Strauss collected a short song book of such lyrics from his classmates; his version contains the following lines not found in our original version: "Do they make a rustic clamor, when you hit them with a hammer?/ Can you bounce them off the wall, like an Indian (sic) rubber ball?/ Do they have a salty taste when you wrap them with your waste (sic)?/ Do they have a hollow sound when you drag them on the ground?/ Do they have a mellow tingle, when you hit them with a shingle?"

    We also ran across adult versions of this song. From *The Dirty Song Book* the following variant lines were found: "Do they have a salty taste when you wrap 'em 'round your waist?/ Do they chime like a gong when you pull upon your dong?" as well as an entirely different verse: "Ting-aling, God damn, find a woman if you can./ If you can't find a woman, find a clean old man./ If you're ever in Gibraltar, take a flying f___ at Walter./ Can you do the double shuffle when your balls hang low?" This second verse, summing up a soldier's traditional lament, imply that this verse did indeed have a military origin. Moreover, the mentions of Gibraltar and the "India rubber ball" suggest the British army and, if the "India rubber" verse is part of the original, the verse must have originated no earlier than the 1870s.

37. Here is a classic "castration-anxiety" rhyme, sung long before the Bobbitt case of early 1994 created a whole bevy of new and raunchy folk jokes. This is a "boys only" song, never to be sung before girls!

38. This matter-of-fact description of overly enthusiastic sex is, of course, a parody of an arithmetics drill, and like all parodies it is easy to remember (possibly easier than the original drill!).

39. This rhyme, for all its intricacy—or perhaps because of it—has traveled around the country for the last twenty or so years. This is the earliest date we've found for it. Whether or not it originated in 1966 or in New York City isn't clear. There's a matter-of-fact acceptance of the sex act as an "occupation" necessary for reproduction that seems strangely passionless—until that final joke ending.

40. There's a blatant play on words in the first line of this version ("boy meets girl"), and an equally blatant invitation in the last—one that, as in the previous version, isn't meant in earnest.

41. This variant omits the lead-in couplet and gets straight to the "action." The last line has changed from the almost polite to the downright forceful "Lie down, sucker." It's understandable that the informant wished to remain anonymous: like a woman overhearing a men-only ritual, she had learned a "forbidden" song.

42. Here is an example of youthful, mild, but very real sexual harassment. The informant was very firm on the point that the older (by two years) boy, a neighbor she disliked, forced her to listen to this rhyme against her will. She apparently later got her revenge on him by punching him on the school bus!

43. We have included this variant primarily for the last line, which brings in the Board of Education and the relatively recent (within the last ten years) furor over sex education in the schools. Some children, obviously, had already figured out a good deal on their own, and didn't mind taking a jab at those who wanted to lecture them.

CHAPTER THREE

1. For more general gross-outs, those not aimed at demystifying any bodily functions but intended purely to disgust, see Chapter One.

2. This gentle little rhyme is rather rare and may be local; the authors have, to date, collected no similar version elsewhere in the country.

3. "Dixie," that quintessential song of the South, was written in 1860 by Daniel Decatur Emmett. What's unusual about most of the "smelly feet" parodies set to the same tune is that they are as likely to mention the singer's own feet as to insult those of others. However, while Version One is surprisingly self-deprecating, Version Two manages to turn the rhyme into a definite, acted-out insult. For more insults, see Chapter Four.

4. A common motif in folklore is the supernatural power of bad smells emanating from a person. In this case, the child singing the rhyme is actually boasting about his or her stench, turning what should be a liability into an asset.

5. This rhyme, which is always chanted rather than sung, has a distinguished pedigree: No less a personage than the sixth century B.C. Greek scholar Pythagoras recommended the eating of beans for good health. Version Three has an oddly occult touch in the third line, with that "the more you wish," although that line, corrupted in the folklore process, probably means only that "the more you eat beans, the more you wish to eat beans." Version Four, however, warns that there can be a side effect to eating too many beans!

6. Farts powerful enough to destroy property are common in the folk rhymes of children, but they are also the subject of much down-to-earth adult folk humor around the world. It's only in more genteel cultures that the passing of gas becomes a taboo subject. However, not all American adults are squeamish about the subject. As renowned a public figure as Benjamin Franklin has, in "A Letter to a Royal Academy" (1781) (published in a collection titled *Fart Proudly* edited by Carl Japikse, Columbus, Ohio: Enthea Press, 1990), made fun of the attempts to cover up a natural function with overly polite euphemisms. Another version of "I was going down the highway," in which the supposed vehicle blown apart by the fart is a train, was collected in Indiana in 1970 and recorded by Simon J. Bronner in *American Children's Folklore*. Fatty and Skinny turn up in a good many American folk rhymes on different themes, as they have for the last hundred years. For more examples, see Chapter Four. For more about "fartlore," see pages 211-16 in *One Potato, Two Potato: The Folklore of American Children*, by Mary and Herbert Knapp. Although the authors, frustratingly, don't cite dates, locations or informant's names and ages, they do give an interesting overview of the

various games and traditions.

The Opies collected a counting rhyme calling for a doctor involving a question-and-answer format in *I Saw Esau: The Schoolchild's Pocket Book* (a revised version of *I Saw Esau: Traditional Rhymes of Youth from 1947*). Again, frustratingly, Iona Opie does not list which rhymes are new to the volume, and which from 1947. Another counting rhyme similar to the Opies' can be found in *Anna Banana*.

7. "How Dry I Am," written in 1921 by Phillip Dodridge and Edward F. Rimbault as a joking protest against Prohibition, has been converted by children ever since into this parody. While a good many versions exist, all of them stress a child's urgent "I really gotta go!" and the panic of possibly not getting there in time. A popular maker of disposable diapers parodied this song as well, implying that their product was superior in keeping the baby dry; it almost certainly helped keep the tune in children's memories and to keep it associated not with a desire to drink but to eliminate. The inclusion in Version Four of this folk rhyme of "Playtex pants" manages to parody the commercial as well! A version with slightly different scansion can be found in *Miss Mary Mack*.

8. This rhyme about toilet training and its attending problems, is amusing to children—and possibly to exasperated parents as well. It is one of the few children's folk rhymes to come with a definite title.

9. This precautionary verse is sometimes quoted by adults as well; it has been written down in one form or another on "whimsical" souvenir plaques. British school graffiti from the 1950s and American folk wisdom still being quoted adds a laconic: "Don't matter how you shake your peg/ The last few drops run down your leg."

10. What makes these two "Sally" versions interesting is that Jerry and Tom are, respectively, father and son. While Tom probably learned it originally from his father, the folk process altered it into a new version. A similar version to our Version Two featuring "Lydia" is found in the chorus of "The Sexual Life of the Camel" in *The Dirty Song Book* compiled by Jerry Silverman.

11. We weren't sure exactly how to classify this one. This parody of Longfellow's famous poem can obviously refer to regurgitation, urination, or defecation. Author Sherman remembers two lines of a variant, "Listen, my children, and you shall hear/ Of the midnight attack of diarrhea," which seems to give the vote to defecation. For more on Jason, see Chapter Three, Note 14.

12. One of the main points of all gross-out rhymes is to present the most revolting ideas possible. As if the idea of seeing the results of diarrhea or even getting it on one's finger wasn't disgusting enough, "The Rasberry Song" adds graphic sound effects; Version Two adds coprophagy to

guarantee the hearer's "eeeuuuwww" response!

13. Not only does this song parody the anxiety of trying to make it to the toilet in time, as do some of the rhymes in this chapter about urination, it adds the fun of mocking a too-frequent commercial jingle as well. For more parodies of commercial products see Chapter Seven.

14. Besides parodying "My Bonnie Lies Over the Ocean" (which is a common target of other, unrelated parodies such as those in the following section on illness) and, in the case of Version Three, parodying cheerleading chants in general, the point of these rhymes is to induce nausea (or at least feigned nausea) in the listener. The informant for Version Three told us extra "points" were scored if the revolted listener was an adult! See also the "Hasten, Jason" lines appended to the "Paul Revere" parody. This is a typical aspect of the folk process, in which bits of one song or story get attached to another. See also Chapter Two.

15. This rhyme, which parodies the 1911 song by Irving Berlin from the show *Everybody's Doing It*, combines the childhood delight of challenging the adult prohibition on picking one's nose with the gross-out delight of suggesting eating a revolting substance. This is not the only tune for this, however. Another, almost identical variant from an unfortunately unidentified source on an electronic bulletin board stated that it should be "sung vaguely to the tune of 'Turkey Trot.'"

16. Although tuberculosis is still very much a threat to public health, even in North America, it is no longer the widespread horror it was only a few decades ago. And yet, despite this fact, the disease retains a firm hold in children's folk rhymes, even among those children who have only a vague idea of what type of disease it is. The use of the term "tuberculosis," rather than the earlier "consumption" dates this rhyme to no earlier than the first half of this century. Dentine, cited in Version One, is, of course, a popular brand of "healthy" chewing gum in the United States. Version Three is yet another example of how the folk process sometimes combines two different rhymes. See Chapter Two, Chapter Eight, and the previous verses on regurgitation in this chapter.

17. Children take a self-defensive delight in such horrifying images as a living body literally falling apart. There are, as these two versions show, many a verse to this rhyme, which is set to the 1938 popular song, "Jealousy," words by Vera Bloom, music by Jacob Gade. Another, somewhat less common variant is to be sung to the Beatles' 1965 song, "Yesterday." Unfortunately, the informant, Adam, who learned it in the late 1960s in Honesdale, Pennsylvania, could only recall the following couplet: "Leprosy … All my parts are falling off of me …" However, this couplet neatly sums up the point of the rhyme! Songwriter/humorist Tom Lehrer wrote his own version of a leprosy song in the 1960s.

18. Rather than mocking a disease, this rhyme celebrates an all-too common accident: people have, indeed, picked bouquets including poison ivy, or even, in at least one unhappy case known to a friend of author Sherman's, used the leaves during a camping trip in lieu of toilet paper!

19. This rhyme has been popular, in these and similar versions, in North America for at least a hundred years. It combines the traditional folk song style of repetition of key phrases—which facilitates memorization—with the warning drummed into many a child: Don't eat anything picked up from the floor or street. What makes Version One noteworthy is the eerie ending, which combines "it was all a dream" with the implication that the singer is caught in an endless loop, a horrifying prospect, too, for those listening to this endless shaggy peanut song. Version Two adds a warning against swearing. Version Three continues with a familiar folkloric motif, that of the soul that cannot gain access to Heaven or Hell and therefore must return to Earth, but gets the singer out of the endless loop by giving away the fatal peanut. One informant, Judy, contributed two lines, ca. 1960s, Connecticut:

    Saw St. Peter, saw St. Peter, saw St. Peter just now,/ Just now I saw St. Peter, saw St. Peter just now,/ and: Saw the Devil, saw the Devil, saw the Devil just now,/ Just now I saw the Devil, saw the Devil just now.

    Another informant, Beth, late 1950s, central Ohio, also knew the "basic" song.

20. For more on the subject of children's parodies of commercial products, see Chapter Seven.

21. In addition to parodying both the idea of suicide and Remco's perfectly innocent game, Versions One and Two also parody the warnings of parents to children about the dangers of suffocation from plastic bags. In an example of the folk process in action, the more recent Versions Three and Four lose the connection with the original game (except for the one line from the commercial) but keep the suicide theme; they seem to reflect some of the horrific stories of suicides related by the news media. The rhyme has also been cited by Matt Groening in his "Life in Hell" series of cartoons.

22. "The Worms Crawl In" or, as it is also known, "The Hearse Song," which, despite its singsong melody is usually sung in a creepy voice, is in its many variations one of the most wide-spread rhymes in North America, continuing its popularity among even those children who have no idea what pinochle is. Needless to say, so wide-spread a rhyme has been collected by other folklorists. See, for example, the versions collected in the 1970s from Delaware and Utah recorded in Simon Bronner's *American Children's Folklore* (op. cit), while Scott E. Hastings, Jr., in his *Miss Mary Mac All Dressed in Black* records one from Vermont. The Pogues (an Irish folk/rock group) recorded a partial variant called

"Worms" on their 1988 album *If I Should Fall From Grace with God* (Island Records).

Why should this be such a popular rhyme? What could possibly be more wonderfully revolting to a child (and downright revolting to an adult) than a graphic description of the body's dissolution—with a comparison to rancid food? These rhymes also parody etiquette instructions: how to eat food, eat three meals a day, and other restrictions on eating what children must eat. In short, this class of rhyme isn't just gross, it's subversive. We could discuss Freudian implications in these rhymes as well, but we won't!

We also heard a great many partial versions in the preparation of the book from people of all ages, including both authors. Versions One adds a line from the classic "Greasy, Grimy Gopher Guts" rhyme: "And I forgot my spoon." For more on "Gopher Guts" and other gross-out rhymes, see Chapter One. Version Three is unusual in that it begins with a folkloric warning about not mocking the dead lest the mocker be punished by death, and ends on a pious note. Version Five, as with Versions One and Three, adds the not uncommon folkloric element of eating thoroughly disgusting, all but unthinkable substances—in this case adding an auto-cannibalistic aspect as well! Version Four is the only one we've seen that features those "little green bugs." Freudians may delight in the fact that they "crawl out your fly." Version Six has an even weirder twist: those "little green bugs" become "little green men" instead, adding an unexpected element of UFOlogy and further cause for delight for the Freudians. Most versions involve pinochle, but we also collected a version involving Parcheesi from Andy in Brooklyn, ca. 1960. Cole and Calmenson have a version with tiddlywinks in *Miss Mary Mack*. Version Seven, obviously only a partial version, adds the surreal imagery of a coffin flying by. It is the only version we've seen that includes the "blood into sauerkraut" element. Version Eight has completely replaced the worms with ants, and is almost unique in having been turned into an out-and-out insult rhyme.

23. This children's magic rite is as arcane a ritual as anything to be found in adult grimoires—or magic shows—and as full of symbolism whose meaning has been lost.

SECTION TWO

1. Legman opines that breaking taboos only works "if the listener is emotionally involved in the matter; [it is essential] that he or she believe in the relevant taboo, and, at some level be afraid of it." Perhaps the reason why the sharing of subversive verse among children is not indicative of any

deep psychiatric dysfunction is because children aren't yet deeply emotionally invested in society's taboos. On the contrary, these verses serve to *define* society's taboos for the young.

CHAPTER FOUR

1. Note that this lack of verses runs contrary to Freudian explanations of dirty jokes as espoused by Renatus Hartogs in *Four-Letter Word Games: The Psychology of Obscenity* and, to a lesser extent, by G. Legman in *Rationale of the Dirty Joke.*

2. Bosco, like Ovaltine, was a chocolate drink meant to be mixed with milk. No matter what they might feel about the product, children gleefully parodied the cheerful commercial—and safely got out a fair amount of hidden resentments at maternal restrictions and rules at the same time. In an odd little reversal, Lawrence, from Long Island, New York, and about twenty years younger than Bruce, remembers hearing his mother sing this rhyme, possibly remembering it from her own childhood.

3. There are dozens of verses in children's folklore that feature Fatty and Skinny as protagonists; see also the "farting" version in Chapter One. Scott Hastings, Jr. recorded two similar versions collected in the early 1970s in Vermont in his *Miss Mary Mac All Dressed in Black.* A similar insult rhyme to a male and female couple is known to author Weisskopf: "Here comes the groom, skinny as a broom./ Here comes the bride, all fat and wide." With new technologies, folklore gets transmitted in new ways, one of the oddest perhaps being the following version—printed on the waist band of Huggies brand diapers! Besides "Jack and Jill," "Farmer in the Dell," and the ABC song, can be found this rhyme: "Two little monkeys jumping on the bed./ One fell off and broke his head./ Mama called the doctor,/ Doctor said: No more monkeys jumping on the bed." The image of a fat and a skinny friend getting into various mishaps turns up in adult popular entertainment, too, the comic team of Laurel and Hardy being a case in point.

4. Children's insult rhymes often compare the victim to a monster, frequently Frankenstein. Version One implies, however, that even though the victim looks as frightening as Frankenstein, he becomes a figure of cartoon mockery when he dances. Porky Pig is, of course, the gentle, laughable, and plump cartoon creation of Warner Brothers. In contrast, Version Two plays up the horror element for all that it's worth.

5. The "Roto Rooter" jingle is still being used by the drain-clearing company of the same name. As with the rhymes comparing an unpopular child to Frankenstein, this version compares him or her to a monster, this time one from outer space. The end verse is not changed from original

commercial, and the parody lies in its juxtaposition with the revised verses of the "Tobar" theme. For more on parodies of commercials and television show themes, see Chapters Seven and Eight.

6. Once again, the idea of eating an unpleasant substance turns up in a children's rhyme. This one adds a touch of titillation with that "bubbles in your underwear."

7. Flatulence—or farting—is, as noted in Chapter One, a common subject for children's rhymes. It is a particularly popular subject when it can be used as part of a specific insult rhyme. A similar version was collected in 1975 in Delaware and was recorded by Simon Bronner in *American Children's Folklore*.

8. There really was an old grey mare, a Standardbred trotter who raced during the nineteenth century. Her owner kept her going on the racing circuit well into her teens (and past her racing prime), hence the rather rueful song. This historical background hasn't stopped children unfamiliar with the original song from turning the melody into the tune for this parody. A version of this rhyme, collected in 1970 from a seven year old boy in Fort Wayne, Indiana, was recorded by Simon Bronner in his *American Children's Folklore*. For more about the use of "The Old Grey Mare" as the melody for children's parodies, see Chapter Eight. Children's insult rhymes often feature the victim's underwear, or lack thereof. See, for instance, other examples in this chapter. Polar bears sometimes make an unexpected predatory appearance in insult rhymes, even in regions where they never appear in fact, possibly as imports from nature books or fairy tales.

9. "Joy to the World" is, of course, part of George Handel's famous composition, *The Messiah*. This religious melody has been turned into secular parodies in various incarnations by children, though this version, aimed at a specific child target, is surely the most vicious. See also variants concerning teachers in Chapter Five, the groundhog in Chapter Six, and Barney in Chapter Nine.

10. These all seem to be verses used by girls teasing other girls. While Version One is a straightforward accusations that a child has a bad odor, Version Two uses the secondary meaning of "dirty" as obscene in a mild play on words that presumably involved a fair amount of giggling amid the counting-out. Version Four keeps the sexual content—in fact, strengthens it a touch—while adding sloth, gluttony, and theft to the list of sins, plus an assertion of insanity. Parents might take some small comfort in the equation of education with liberation! As in Version Five, the strenuous disavowal of the kiss might be a defense against accusations of lesbianism. It is possible that Version Five takes the form of a back and forth rhyme for two people. It also adds the vice of nosiness to the mix, brings in popular showman/pianist Liberace to rhyme with "scotch,"

"Halloweenie" to rhyme with "eenie," and turns the kiss into a raspberry. Such nonsense phrases as "Eenie meeny pop-sa-leenie" are very common in children's hand clapping and jump rope rhymes. While they definitely help keep the beat going, whether or not they are all corruptions of actual words or phrases is open to debate.

The trick contrary ending of Version Four, that emphatic, sarcastic "Not!" definitely dates this form of the rhyme to the 1990s. Version Six is a somewhat bizarre twist of a very popular children's rhyme, "Miss Mary Mac," which usually features a quite innocent young lady borrowing some money to see an elephant (or elephants) jump a fence. See, for instance, Scott E. Hastings, Jr.'s *Miss Mary Mac All Dressed in Black*. However, in the very recent version we record here, the innocent has become a pipe-smoking illiterate going to see what sounds suspiciously like a male strip show! Note also Versions Three and Four use a couplet more often heard in the "Miss Lucy" rhymes found in Chapter Two.

11. The idea of a child sticking his or her head in some highly unpleasant or at least unlikely substance is a common feature of children's insult rhymes. Version One is certainly the most straightforward of the two, but Version Two is a bit more sophisticated in its "send you to the Navy" line. This doesn't refer to any specific war or other event, just to the idea of exiling a child. Note however, that the informant heard this during the Vietnam years, when the military was not in high in the public esteem. A version almost the same as our Version Two can be found in Cole and Calmenson's *Miss Mary Mack*. A version somewhat similar was collected in 1968 from Indiana and can be found in Simon Bronner's *American Children's Folklore*.

12. This rhyme undoubtedly succeeded in getting a child's attention! It most definitely was not meant for adult overhearing.

13. The main point of this type of rhyme is to win by insulting the other combatant so badly he (or, much more rarely, she) can't retort and has to back down without any physical blows being exchanged.

14. Trigger was the palomino horse of Roy Rogers, the most famous movie cowboy of the fifties and sixties.

15. The "wheet" noise mentioned in the second verse from this informant probably refers to a sound commonly found on several hit rap records of the late 1980s. Note also the association of the long-running public television program Sesame Street with urban life. The idea of insulting someone's mother or grandmother by calling them prostitutes is a common street insult. Similar references to the use of such hair care products as Afro-Sheen in the first verse, can be found in Snaps,, which primarily contains examples of black children insulting each other. Grissom High School, however, is almost entirely attended by whites. Students there may have used such chants or "anti-cheers" during sporting events to

provoke an emotional response from competitors that might lead to a bad play. Offensive as it is, this strategy is commonly encountered in all American sports, from a catcher in little league distracting a batter with taunts about his sister, to a professional football lineman conversing with his opposite number about his excessive weight or lack of manliness.

16. This is a very popular jump rope chant, with versions to be found across North America. For instance, Simon Bronner records almost identical versions collected in the 1970s from Maine and Maryland in his *American Children's Folklore* while Francelia Butler, in her *Skipping Around the World*, cites one collected in 1947 from Virginia, and Scott Hastings, Jr. lists in *Miss Mary Mac All Dressed in Black* several versions collected in the 1980s in Vermont. The implied sexual behavior of the child mentioned ties this in with the rhymes in Chapter Two. Scott Hastings, Jr. included a version in which the implied behavior becomes a bit more obvious, since the girls jumping rope were supposed to pull up their dresses to show their slips while jumping.

17. This, like Version One, contains more than a hint of implied sexual behavior, including the split done while reciting the "K.I.S.S." line. The replacement of "policeman" by "mailman" is less common. The informant's description of learning the rhyme by watching other children perform shows a common way that children's folklore is transmitted.

18. Both of these are versions of the "gotcha" genre of folkloric hand motion jokes. In the first rhyme, the first two lines may be a veiled racial insult. Atari is a brand of video entertainment system. Mock karate battles in the schoolyard became popular in the mid-1970s with the television show *Kung Fu* and the hit song *"Kung Fu Fighting"* and have undergone an even more widespread resurgence in the 1990s due to the children's television *Mighty Morphin Power Rangers*; this verse, however, predates the *Power Rangers*, and the violence would not seem to be able to be placed at its door. In the second rhyme, "Coke" is used in the South as a generic term for all carbonated drinks. The idea of Chinese people adulterating food may be tied into the urban legend of Chinese restaurants secretly using rodents and pets, especially cats, in their dishes (Jan Harold Brunvand, *The Choking Doberman and Other "New" Urban Legends*). Both the verse, with its pidgin English grammar, and the actions, with the hands held together in front of the body, play on stereotypes of Chinese.

19. The authors have seen fights—both verbal and physical—break out among spectators during baseball games, and deaths have occurred during soccer matches.

20. "We Will Rock You" (written in 1977 by Freddie Mercury), recorded by the rock group Queen, has been used as a fight song at many a sports event, so it's not at all surprising that children should have picked it up and turned it into their own. Their versions start as challenging boasts,

then turn personal, Version One with the threat of stealing underwear (the Freudians might see this as symbolic of a sexual assault), Version Two ending with a child's secret dread of losing control of his/her bowels.

21. "Ta-Ra-Ra-Boom-Der-Ay" was written in 1891 by Englishman Henry J. Sayers, but quickly acclimated itself in the United States as well. Still, although many of our informants knew the title, few of them spelled it like the original. What makes this particular rhyme interesting is not only the standard attack on an enemy child's underwear—with the deliciously titillating idea of leaving that child naked—but the tie-in to the very old folk motif of "The Master Thief," the character, found throughout the world, who is a clever enough thief to steal the pants right off a victim.

22. Along with a child's fascination with underwear and the hint of sexual matters involved in the stealing or vanishing of the same, is an almost equal fascination with excretion, as was discussed in Chapter Three, and with the flushing away of waste, whether actual or implied. The game of tag described here, known as Flush, provides the children playing it with the thrill of possibly ending up as "It," symbolic human waste—to say nothing of safely letting out resentment against those "Its" a child really disliked.

23. Author Sherman adds that no, the fifth graders did not add a line about themselves, or about the students in older grades. "Third grade angels" was intended not as a compliment, but as a "goody-goody" insult.

24. For more about songs that, through clever twists, never quite turn dirty, except in the listener's mind, see the examples in Chapter Two.

25. The War of the Sexes starts at an early age, though sociologists may ponder on how much of the animosity is sociological rather than genetic. A variant of Version One collected in 1972 in Utah was recorded by Simon Bronner in *American Children's Folklore*, while Scott Hastings, Jr. recorded a good many variants throughout Vermont in the early 1970s, which he listed in *Miss Mary Mac All Dressed in Black*. Most of Bronner and Hastings' versions end with the two mothers getting into a fist fight. Scott Hastings also collected a variant of Version Two in the early 1970s in Vermont. Note also the additional verse to Version Five of "Eeny Meeny Miney Moe."

26. A discerning reader must surely have noticed that Version One soon leaves the tune far behind. Not only is this rhyme a catalogue of all the things parents dread, from drugs to sex, it adds the section about "Granny" on the outhouse door, which is an add-on from another song sometimes attached to parodies. Version Two has more somber undertones than Version One, what with its strong references to child abuse and the singer's fear about going home. Regarding Version Two, Scott Hastings, Jr. records a similar version collected in the early 1970s in

Vermont. For other parodies of "Yankee Doodle" see Chapter Eight.

27. The stereotypical image of the dumb blond is an old one in America, but it has come into its own in the last decade or so as the center of a cycle of joke-lore. What makes this of particular interest to folklorists is the fact that a good many of these "dumb blond" jokes are identical to those previously told about the equally stereotypical Jewish-American Princess; while the so-called "J.A.P." jokes are gradually going out of fashion since they are considered at least marginally anti-Semitic, jokesters have taken these jests and turned instead to a group unallied to any one race or creed (save for the fact that dumb blonds in these jokes are almost always female). For more on this folkloric process, see Chapter Nine of author Sherman's *A Sampler of Jewish-American Folklore*.

28. "Happy Birthday to You" was written in 1893 and copyrighted in 1935 by Patty Smith Hill and Mildred J. Hill, who certainly never suspected that their very popular and decidedly upbeat song would be the basis for these and similar decidedly downbeat parodies. Simon Bronner records two more from 1960s Indiana in his *American Children's Folklore*, but there are many others being sung by children all across North America. And, in the case of the "Volga Boatman" version, by adults too.

29. Several versions of the more sentimental Version One (and one satiric variant) have been collected from the 1960s through the 1980s from Delaware, New Jersey, Pennsylvania, and Indiana and recorded in Simon Bronner's *American Children's Folklore*. Others, some nice, some not, are cited, unfortunately without sources, by Mary and Herbert Knapps in their *One Potato, Two Potato*. Variations spell the character's name as "Cee Cee" or even, as in Version Two, "Say Say."

30. The sort of non sequitur, almost-Dadaist humor found in this rhyme is just as popular with adults as with children. Such slogans as "American Non Sequitur Society: We don't make sense, but we do like pizza," have been seen by both authors.

31. While these four versions parody the Victorian style of formal recitation popular in this country, this type of "impossible" or "contrary" story is very old, indeed; Versions One and Two, with their hints of deeper, arcane rituals, have their roots in early Medieval—and possibly pre-Christian—Europe. Peter and Iona Opie record two versions in *I Saw Esau* and trace these back to 1480.

"Contrary" themes exist in such folksongs as the British "The Darby Ram," Stephen Foster's "Oh, Susanna," and in such societies as the Contraries of the Lakota people, who traditionally do everything in reverse from the norm. Version Five has definitely been affected by the informant's locale, with that unique "Mississisloppy." Two versions of "Ladies and gentlemen" that don't include the "two dead boys" recitation were collected in 1982 in Pennsylvania and are recorded in Simon

Bronner's *American Children's Folklore*. Scott E. Hastings, Jr. recorded a version of "two dead boys" collected in the early 1970s in Vermont in his *Miss Mary Mac All Dressed in Black*.

CHAPTER FIVE

1. "The Battle Hymn of the Republic" was written in 1862 by Julia Ward Howe and William Steffe utilizing the melody of an old religious song, and has been the subject of innumerable parodies by American children ever since, possibly because the words and melody are so memorable. Although there are parodies that fit the melody for the stanzas and that of the chorus (i.e., the lines beginning, "Glory, Glory, Hallelujah") only three of the versions we collected, Versions Four, Five, and Six, were meant by the informants to be sung together as one unit. This is in marked contrast to those versions, collected around the United States mostly during the 1960s and 1970s, listed in Simon J. Bronner's *American Children's Folklore*, which do combine both "halves" into one "whole" song. We have chosen to organize them as the informants gave them to us.

2. For another example of World War II survivals in folk rhyme, see the informant's "Sleep, baby, sleep" in Chapter Seven.

3. This is clearly a rhyme about the reaction of children to corporal punishment, but in the North at least, it is a historical carry over; corporal punishment was unknown in the New York City public schools at the time author Weisskopf first heard the rhyme. In the South, however, things are different. Author Weisskopf was shocked to discover in the seventh grade, after her family had made the move to the South, that Alabama public schools were more old fashioned, and that the rhyme was actually commenting on reality. Author Weisskopf recalls from her time in Brooklyn a whole series of variations using colors (rhyming "purple" with "girdle" for instance), but these were probably made up on the spot, as with "ranks" (also known as "snaps"). The rhyme has a deeper implication, that "corporal punishment" results in "capital punishment."

4. The one constant in these versions is the figure of that menacing teacher—and the ever increasing (and increasingly improbable) firepower used by the student to retaliate.

5. For other children's parodies using this melody, see Chapters Four and Eight. "On Top of Old Smokey," an Appalachian folk song, has an odd history. One modern adaptation was copyrighted in 1951 by Pete Seeger, while a parody of that version, "On Top of Spaghetti," was written and copyrighted in 1963 by Tom Glazer. The folk process being what it is, parodies of both songs have spread throughout the country; we have

omitted those variants that were specifically based on the copyrighted songs as not really being in the public domain (many informants were astonished to learn that "On Top of Spaghetti" really is a copyrighted song), and restricted ourselves to parodies based on the original folk song. See also the similar versions collected in the 1970s and early 1980s from Indiana, Delaware, and Pennsylvania recorded in Simon Bronner's *American Children's Folklore*. The anti-teacher rhyme that follows those above features a submarine that may be another relic of World War II, as does Version Two of "Glory, Glory Hallelujah." It also features that "I bopped her on the bean" line common to several versions of "Glory, Glory Hallelujah."

6. As noted in Chapter Four, wherein Handel's "Joy to the World" was used as an insult against another child, this song has been used by children in their parodies in many ways. A good many versions feature the rather grisly element of getting rid of the body by flushing it down the toilet. See as well the "Groundhog" song in Chapter Six, and the anti-Barney rhyme in Chapter Nine.

7. Here is another example of a cheerful Christmas carol turned into an equally cheerful anti-school parody. Version One is a bit more gentle than the norm, dealing with vandalism rather than outright violence against teacher, principal, and school. On the other hand, these are all occurrences that can happen, whereas actually killing teachers, as suggested in the parodies of "The Battle Hymn of the Republic," isn't at all common. As a recipe, this verse is more subversive than mere ironic exaggerations. Version Two parodies the carol, but also jokes about arson and mocks parental warnings about matches as well. Simon Bronner, in his *American Children's Folklore*, cites an almost identical version collected in 1985 from a nine-year-old girl from Harrisburg, Pennsylvania.

8. This counting out rhyme, variously spelled "Eeny meeny miney moe" or "eenie meenie miney moe," started out as a racial slur, and then was softened as public awareness changed. This anti-teacher version returns to the original intent, but takes the insult in new directions. See Chapter Six for examples of both the pre- and post-Civil Rights Era versions of the non-teacher-oriented counting out rhyme.

9. "Row, Row, Row Your Boat" is a very well-known folk round. This parody falls into the category of a "gotcha," starting out with deceptive mildness, then switching suddenly to an anti-teacher theme. Version Two includes the "Delaware" rhyme usually associated with attacks not on teachers but on other children. For more trips down the Delaware and problems with predatory polar bears, see Chapter Three.

10. It is somehow very fitting to see this commercial jingle turned into a parody. Chiquita Banana, the cartoon character who personifies a brand of banana (a trademark developed in 1944 by the United Fruit Company), is

in her own right a parody of the late singer and dancer, Carmen Miranda. The trademark became widely known due to a song released by Miranda and bandleader Xavier Cugat. A similar version can be found in *Miss Mary Mack*. For more children's parodies of commercial jingles, see Chapter Seven.

11. For political parodies of the 1937 song "Whistle While You Work," see Chapter Six. The original, written by Larry Morey and Frank Churchill, comes from the Walt Disney full-length cartoon feature, *Snow White and the Seven Dwarfs*.

12. This nicely tongue-in-cheek song of defiance seems to be a good place to leave the subject of tormenting teachers, with the children determined to keep fighting.

13. As the school year winds down, a good many teachers, as well as most students, count down the months, weeks, days, and even hours till freedom! In *I Saw Esau* the Opies collected in Maryland in 1947 the more traditional children's cry on the last day of school: "No more pencils, no more books,/ No more teacher's sassy looks." Author Weisskopf would substitute "dirty" for "sassy," however.

14. Sometimes a child's rhyme will pay a twisted, backhanded compliment to the teacher! No one would believe that nuns really were brewing beer down in the school's basement, but it must have been fun for the students to pretend they were reprobates. Still, it might have been a reference to the stereotype of the Catholic priest as drunkard. And certain Catholic religious orders have become famous for their beer and wine.

15. The Notre Dame fight song, like all school songs, is full of upbeat optimism about the status of the school and the valor of its students. As a result, it is an easy target for parody by students who really don't care to be forced into the mold of "perfect little ladies or gentlemen." There actually is a good deal of underage drinking in North America, as statistics show, but it certainly isn't as widespread as this cheerful parody implies.

16. The late 1960s and early 1970s were the heyday of "recreational" pharmaceuticals, as is reflected in these songs. Even children who had no intention of trying drugs knew about marijuana and the hallucinogen known as LSD. Version Two adds a political note, though of course neither the late New York Governor Nelson Rockefeller nor former Mayor John Lindsay had anything at all to do with the drug trade.

17. Version One refers, of course, to the American Communist Party; this rhyme manages to combine a school and political parody in one. For more political parodies, see Chapter Six. Judging from the EPA's report cited by the informant, Version Two might actually have had some justification! Mount Holyoke is a very prestigious woman's college in South

Hadley, Massachusetts. Its prestige, however, didn't stop its students from turning the noble school song into something else entirely. And the process still continues: today's students frequently refer to the town as "How Sadly!"

18. This is yet another example of an upright, decent school song—which of course makes it a perfect target for parodying. Notice all three versions share the opening lines—although none of the informants were classmates or even all attendees of the same school. Folklore, as has been noted before, travels.

19. This is, of course, a parody not just of school songs but of the superhuman purity expected (originally in Victorian times) from students—at least in fiction. It dates at least to the early years of this century. A version of this rhyme was part of "The Battle of Kookamunga," a 1959 Grammy winner about a Boy Scout troop sung by the parodists Homer & Jethro (which was itself a parody of "The Battle of New Orleans," the even-bigger song by Johnny Horton about the War of 1812).

20. The original adult version which they parodied so effectively implies that those scouts do so many good deeds that they are lauded by everyone they meet, yet remain modest and wholesome.

21. "Alma Mater" is a traditional tune used by many schools and organizations as the melody for their "theme" songs.

22. This is another "take" on the adults' idealized image of the too-nice camper being totally mangled by a children's parody that shows campers as hard-living, rough-talking, and every parent's nightmare.

23. These two parodies were meant to be sung as brightly as any vaudeville songs. Author Sherman has a vague memory of hearing a version in the 1970s in New York City, but can recall only the two lines that begin Version One.

24. "Rock-in Robin," a song about a Rock and Roll loving bird, was written in 1958 by Jimmie Thomas. It reached number two on the pop charts twice, once in 1958 sung by Bobby Day and again in 1972 (as "Rockin' Robin") sung by Michael Jackson. What is typical of this and similar parodies is that they are just as likely to be sung by children raised as Christians as by those raised in any other faiths or no faith at all; it's much more daring to mock the conventions of one's own religion, after all.

25. The lyrics to the Sunday school hymn "Jesus Loves You" were written by Anna Bartlett Warner in 1859, the tune by William B. Bradbury in 1862. It contains the lines, "Little ones to Him belong,/ They are weak but he is strong." The little ones are mean too. In 1955 there was a hit tune called "The Bible Tells Me So."

26. This chilling little ditty sounds like a miniature horror story or perhaps

the basis of a murder mystery, and may conceivably have been inspired by some older song or tale a child happened to hear.

27. For other nonsense rhymes and examples of intricate doubletalk, see Chapter Four.

CHAPTER SIX

1. Just how old is this verse? In its current form, featuring a Girl or Boy Scout, it can't date back further than 1908, when Scouting began in this country, but it may conceivably have older roots in the previous century. Version One is the most common. Author Weisskopf's version was used as a counting rhyme in conjunction with "Eenie Meenie Miney Moe" and another verse usually sung by boys: "Raquel Welch, she's the best./ She's got mountains on her chest." Version Two is unusual in that the rhyme is turned into a racial slur, replacing "soldier" with "nigger." This was the only such example of this verse that we've collected, although racial slurs certainly do turn up with greater frequency in counting-out rhymes such as the "Eenie Meenie" versions we recorded later in this chapter. Version Three definitely reflects World War II, twenty or so years after the war ended. This survival isn't too unusual; there are a good many such rhymes still being sung. See the examples later in this chapter. Version Four is both the most modern and the most unusual with its strong sexual implications, the soldier having been turned into a monkey, and the transformation of the rhyme itself into an explicit counting-out rhyme. It is also the most aggressively insulting to the listener. See Chapter Four for more insult rhymes.

2. For another World War II survival recalled by the informant, see his version of "Glory, Glory Hallelujah" in Chapter Six.

3. Although many people think that "The Colonel Bogey March" originated with the movie *The Bridge Over the River Kwai*, it was actually written by Kenneth J. Alford in 1916, and has been the tune for many a World War II children's parody both in England and America. (The "Colonel Bogey" of the title is not a military man, but a golf term for an imaginary partner!)

4. "Whistle While You Work," the Seven Dwarfs theme song in Walt Disney's animated movie, *Snow White* (first released in 1937), was turned into a World War II parody both in North America and in Britain. What is interesting is both that the song in all its versions should have survived nearly forty years after the end of World War II, when the names involved could hardly be of immediate relevance to children, and that the British versions, despite the British having been under direct German attack during the war, tend to be milder than their American

counterparts. Rhymes collected by Iona and Peter Opie, for instance, and featured in *The Lore and Language of Schoolchildren* published in 1959, replace the emphatic American "Hitler is a jerk" with a softer "Hitler (or Mussolini) wore (or made) a shirt." See Version Three for a Canadian example of that milder version. All references to the euphemistic "wee-nie" and the slightly blunter "peenie" appear only in the American versions. Version Four is the only version reported directly from the World War II era, and the only one to make reference to the other front. For another parody of "Whistle While You Work," this time unrelated to World War II, see Chapter Five.

5. Although these parodies reflect the World War II era (even though the idea of Germany having a king, or kaiser, dates back to World War I and before), the Cold War with the former Soviet Union was very much in progress during the 1950s and 1960s, as were stories about spies being caught in the United States; the names of the enemies changed, but the sentiments remained the same. Donald Duck, along with Mickey Mouse and other celebrities, frequently turns up in children's parodies. For more celebrity spots, see Chapters One and Eight; for more versions of "My Country Tis of Thee" see Chapter Eight.

6. The tune of "Casey Jones," written in 1909 by Lawrence Seibert and Eddie Newton, was turned into a commercial jingle in the early 1960s, just in time to be reused in this Cold War era parody. The children singing it might not have always understood all the political ramifications of what they were singing, but that hardly mattered. They knew enough to identify Fidel Castro and Nikolai Khrushchev as "bad guys." For other, less political, parodies of commercial jingles, see Chapter Seven.

7. The first of these two parodies employs the "Mouseketeer" song of the 1950s, known to anyone who has ever seen the *The Mickey Mouse Club* television show (ran 1955-1959). The second uses the tune of "Waltzing Matilda," which was written in 1903 by A.B. Patterson and has pretty much become the unofficial anthem of Australia. Together, they must certainly be among the more unusual of the rhymes that we've collected, and among the most unique. They are two of the very few parodies of Stalin-era communism we've found from North American children.

8. "Peter Cottontail," an innocent, bouncy little song about the coming of the Easter Bunny, was written by Steve Nelson and Jack Rollins, who certainly had no idea it would be turned into a grimly cheerful Cold War parody. Informant Jim in New York reports that he learned this version of the last two lines of "America the Beautiful" in the year of the Cuban missile crisis: "And crown thy guts with Khrushchev's nuts/ From sea to shining sea."

9. "Havah Nagila" is a very popular Hebrew folksong, as everyone who has ever attended a Jewish celebration knows. It is also frequently parodied;

see Chapter Eight for a non-political example.

10. There's a double delight for children who recite this rhyme. Not only do they get to play at adult politics, they also get a chance to end what seems like a perfectly innocuous rhyme with a zinger.

11. According to Bill Bryson in *Made in America*, the counting rhyme "Eeny, Meenie, Minie, Moe" is based on a counting system found in pre-Roman Britain. But the curious can trace the progress of the modern American variants through time and across the country as the word in the second line changed from racial pejorative to the more innocuous "tiger." The word "nigger" became taboo for the most part in the early to mid-1960s in the northern states (there are isolated exceptions), but lingered on in children's rhymes through the 1960s into the early 1970s in the southern states. Nancy, one of our informants, learned the "nigger" version in fourth grade at the National Cathedral School for Girls in Washington, D.C. in 1968; by 1970 the word had changed to "tiger." The informant of Version Six also knew the innocuous "tiger" version, a version using "nigger," a racial slur against black people, and one using "redneck," a term usually applied in a derogatory way to uneducated white Southerners. Southerners will themselves frequently use "redneck" as a slur.

    The substitution of "robber" for "nigger" in Version Two turns the rhyme into something that actually makes sense—the apprehension of a criminal. But how did "tiger" get into the rhyme? That's a mystery of folklore. Tigers do turn up in children's fiction now and again, and presumably made the transfer from prose to rhyme at some point because the word sounds similar to the one it replaces, alliterates nicely, fits the meter, and is familiar to children. However, in one of the weird coincidences of comparative folklore, Chinese folklore, with which most North American children were unfamiliar in the 1960s, features a character named Tiger who is a robber.

12. This type of racist rhyme was still in wide circulation as late as 1970, but is no longer found as often. This doesn't mean racism has disappeared, but rather that children no longer tend to sing about it, or that they sing about it less openly. For more about parodies on commercial jingles including this one, see Chapter Seven.

13. See also the hybrid version in Chapter One, which combines the bedbug baseball game with a variant of "Greasy Grimy Gopher Guts." The Weavers recorded a folk song using the same last two lines as the first verse of Version Two.

14. Although it seems that this carol has been around forever, "We Three Kings of Orient" was actually written in 1857 by John Henry Hopkins. The parody takes the common folkloric form of the cumulative verse, popular examples of which include "The Twelve Days of Christmas" and

"Green Grow the Rushes-O."

15. "Jingle Bells," which was written by J.S. Pierpont in 1857, is the subject of many a child's folk parodies, perhaps because of its simple lyrics and bouncy, easily remembered tune—and because it is played so frequently during the Christmas season. See also those parodies in Chapters Five and Nine. Version Two gets in a jibe at a popular cereal. Version Four manages to combine Santa Claus, Easter, and a popular brand of automobile in a nice bit of non sequitur nonsense. Version Five brings in Halloween and German submarines (similar to rhymes found in Chapter Five in parodies of "The Battle Hymn of the Republic"). Version Six's "shock and shells" is a child's corruption of the more common "shotgun shells." See, for example, the "shotgun shells" versions collected in Utah and Pennsylvania and recorded in Simon Bronner's *American Children's Folklore*.

16. "A Visit from St. Nicholas," written by Clement Clarke Moore and first published in 1823, is certainly one of the best-known Christmas poems of the last two hundred years. It is also frequently parodied by adults as well as children. This particular children's parody may be a shortened version of an adult rhyme; it reflects a child's growing interest in and knowledge of automobiles.

17. "Rudolph the Red-Nosed Reindeer," composed by Johnny Marks, was first published in 1949 and went on to become phenomenally successful, with over three hundred different recordings and over fifty-million records sold. Being so widely popular—and so widely over-played during the Christmas season—it became an obvious target for children's parodies. *Maverick*, mentioned in Version Two, was a popular television Western starring James Garner (ran 1957-1962). For more parodies of songs we all know and of media tunes, see Chapter Eight.

18. This parody manages to combine two favorite themes in children's rhymes: "smelly feet" and with the ever-popular theme of underwear and the threat of its being eaten or removed. For more on the subject of offensive body odors as a subject for children's parodies, see Chapter One. Cole and Calmenson's *Miss Mary Mack* contains several rhymes involving the ingestion of underwear, as in Version Two.

19. At first glance, this is a straight forward gross-out rhyme, but there are some surprising elements here, echoes of ancient animal sacrifice and ritual consumption of the sacrifice that parallel such well-known songs as "Who Killed Cock-Robin?" and the British custom of hunting and sacrificing "the Wren, the Wren, the King of Birds." The archetypes will out! It's a nice coincidence (or—as the historians might wonder—is it truly coincidental?) that Groundhog Day takes place on February 2, the date of the Midwinter Solstice, during which time rituals were (and still are) performed around the world to ensure the return of the sun and the end of winter.

SECTION THREE

1. "Jokes are not invented; they are evolved." G. Legman, *Rationale of the Dirty Joke*, (op. cit. For his discussion of this idea, see pages 26-30.) See also Isaac Asimov's *Treasury of Humor*, and Simon Bronner, *American Children's Folklore*.

2. And, in turn, the commercial world perpetuates folklore. Subversive folk rhymes have been found recently in the cartoons of Matt Groening, and in songs by such diverse popular singers as Christine Lavin, Rickie Lee Jones, and Meat Loaf; even MTV's Beavis and Butthead have been known to let loose with a verse or two.

CHAPTER SEVEN

1. Sometimes children, just like adults, are taken in by advertising, but sometimes they show a surprising amount of buyer resistance. One child known to author Sherman was heard summing up commercials with a contemptuous, "They're just trying to sell you something."

2. McDonald's is, of course, a fast food chain whose advertisements often contain catchy jingles. Two different ad campaigns, "McDonald's is your kind of place," run in the 1970s, and "You deserve a break today," run in the 1980s, inspired a good many parodies. Both are examples of the "boomerang effect": the campaigns were so successful that parodies were widespread too. Versions Four and Five, with their reference to pollution, reflect the ecological movement, which was gaining ground and public awareness in the 1960s. A particularly nice version incorporating polluted eggs, the eating of underwear, and hotdogs, is found in *One Potato, Two Potato*. Note that McDonald's has never served hotdogs.

3. This parody is based on Burger King's "Have it Your Way" campaign. The last line seems a bit unlikely, since the "victim" is already supposed to be at a Burger King, and may be the result of mistaken memory.

    Jay Mechling reports collecting from the Boy Scout troop he studied a version of "Greasy Grimy Gopher Guts" in which the boys would top each other by adding lines to the end, including one "Have it your way, have it your way!" sung as in the Burger King commercial.

4. The Beefaroni jingle had an insistent beat that made it easy for consumers to remember—and easy for children to mock. The product, of course, was perfectly healthy and innocuous, but the combination of that jingle with the look of chopped beef was apparently irresistible to children.
    One of our informants for Version Three knew that it was sung to the tune of the Beefaroni jingle, even though product name is not actually

mentioned in the rhyme.

For more on coprophagy and feces, see Chapter Three. For other gross-outs, see Chapter One.

5. The Oscar Mayer Wiener song (it is copyright Oscar Mayer & Co. 1965) is hard to parody, since it's so full of double entendres to begin with. The solution in this one is to ignore the sexual innuendo and indulge in plain silliness. See also Chapter Six for a parody involving racial slurs and violence.

6. It's margarine.

7. In the original jingle, running in the early 1950s, Nestlé tasted the very best.

8. Bungalow Bar was an ice cream bar. Similar to parodies below, common-sense advice—in this case not to eat too many sweets—gets "de-euphemized."

9. The Tootsie Roll was invented in 1896.

10. While it is not parody of an actual slogan or advertising ditty, Jay Mechling does cite a parody of the Pledge of Allegiance collected from an eleven year old Pennsylvania girl in 1984 which manages to make fun of Pepsi's choice in one ad campaign of Michael Jackson as a spokesman.

11. When Pepsi-Cola first ran the ditty these verses are parodying as part of an ad campaign in the 1930s, its sales doubled. The original verse [if we are allowed to run it] is as follows: "Pepsi-Cola hits the spot;/ Twelve full ounces, that's a lot./ Twice as much for a nickel too./ Pepsi-Cola is the drink for you."

12. For more on ingestion of turpentine, see Chapter Three and the "Lincoln, Lincoln" rhymes.

13. The original advertisement (first aired on television in 1956), began "Winston tastes good/ Like a cigarette should," a lapse of grammar that apparently raised quite a controversy among language purists, generated a fair amount of publicity—and ensured a series of parodies. Version One is relatively mild; Version Two adds a stronger element of gross-out. Version Three is actually a wry joke on the teller. And Version Four refers, of course, to the late English Prime Minister, Winston Churchill, and adds a sophisticated, slightly risque nuance.

14. Harry S. Truman, who was from Missouri, was President from 1945-1953. His daughter Margaret was born in 1924, and has made a name for herself by writing mysteries set in political Washington, D.C. Schlitz is "The Beer That Made Milwaukee Famous," while Budweiser is brewed in St. Louis—there has always been a rivalry between those two great American brewing cities.

15. This is a parody of an ad running on television in New York in the early

1970s inviting tourists to Jamaica—the first use of television to advertise travel destinations. The note of realism is refreshing compared to glamorous images of beautiful people on beaches. In 1969, there were more "skyjackings" than in all the years combined since 1952, when the first plane was hijacked. In 1972, there was an international strike by pilots to bring the issue to the public eye.

16. For more on the subject of ingestion taboos, see Chapter Three.

17. The movie was first released in 1957. Most if not all informants knew the tune and identified the movie as its source. For another verse utilizing the tune, see Chapter Two.

18. Comet is a popular brand of cleanser; countless mothers have warned countless children about the dangers of tasting this and other perilous substances, and so those children have retaliated with this and similar parodies.

    Versions One is the most common that we've seen, involving the one product and its effect on the mouth and teeth. Versions Two is a double-barrelled parody, tackling both Comet and the mouthwash, Listerine, which has probably been thrown in not through any particular hatred for the latter but because it makes a neat rhyme. Similar versions were collected from Janni Lee, who recalled, "It makes your lips turn green," ca. 1980, Long Island, and Jeanne, who remembered, "It tastes like Vaseline," ca. 1980, New Jersey. A slightly tamer version of our Version One is repeated by Jay Mechling in "Children's Folklore" from "Social Interaction Patterns of Adolescents in a Social Performance" by Steve Bartlett, published in *Folklore Forum* in 1971.

19. "Rejex" was the name for any cheap sneakers bought at a five and ten. Pro-Keds and Pumas were the best sneakers to own, preferably in suede—but only the big kids had suede sneakers. In second grade, in that era, no one was mugged for a pair of shoes even though cool sneakers were status objects.

20. Like some of the rhymes about Comet, this verse contains a double-barrelled parody: Elmer's Glue-All is an adhesive often used by children. It also brings in a hint of adult worries in the line, "Ajax will make you pay tax."

21. Both verses show how parodies move along with the times. The first parodies an early Ajax commercial (complete with animated pixies singing those "boom booms") that first aired in 1948, and the later verse parodies a successive commercial, one that featured the statement, "Stronger than dirt," and a White Knight on horseback.

22. The chorus to the original Pepsodent toothpaste jingle (first aired on TV in a commercial in 1956) was "You'll wonder where the yellow went/

When you brush your teeth with Pepsodent." The commercial was a cartoon, and one of the first aimed at teenagers. Also, its very simplicity in rhyme and tune made it an obvious choice for children's parodies.

23. While this verse does hang together suspiciously well, it does not appear to be a composed folk song. The mention of "Grandma's underwear" tends to support its credentials as true folklore, old ladies' underwear being a common theme running throughout many of the rhymes we have collected. Also, the informant is herself a professional folklorist, and she presumably would know!

CHAPTER EIGHT

1. See *Folksongs of Britain and Ireland*, edited by Peter Kennedy, for one well-documented compilation of songs and variants.

2. Folklore is conservative, keeping old forms even while adapting to new circumstances. Perhaps one reason for this is, as these verses exemplify, the tune is memorable but the words easily mutable. Another might be that while circumstances change, human failings remain remarkably constant, so that subversive rhymes can attribute the same faults or excesses to any number of celebrities.

3. These are parodies of the folk song "On Top of Old Smokey," (see Chapter Five on teachers for more). Version One contains a subversive reference to that symbol of sixties uprightness, Dr. Kildare. The show *Dr. Kildare* ran from 1961-1966 and starred Richard Chamberlain as young Dr. Kildare. He was cleanshaven and not noticeably hairy. (Dr. Kildare had an earlier life in feature films of the 1930s and '40s; the character was created by Max Brand in his 1937 story "Interns Can't Take Money.") Betty Grable was a pin-up girl of the World War II era. In Version Two the movie stars embarrassed were: Gene Autry, a famous singing cowboy of the thirties and forties; Roy Rogers, his successor in the fifties and sixties; Marilyn Monroe, a sex symbol of the fifties; and Brigitte Bardot, sex symbol of the late fifties and early sixties.

4. Garbage has the triple attraction of being 1) gross, 2) unsanitary and not to be played with, and 3) demeaning to work with (taboo socially). It's the last thing a tough hero like Popeye would be associated with.

   The character Popeye was created by E.S. Segar; his pipe-smoking, spinach-eating sailor's first appearance was in a print cartoon strip in the 1930s. Popeye then went on to star in black and white animated cartoons made from 1933-1954. These were syndicated on television starting in 1956, and were followed up in 1962 by made-for-television cartoons created by many of the same people as the previous cartoons, including the last actor to do the voice of Popeye, which made for considerable continuity over the more than thirty year history of the cartoon. For instance, all the animated features used Popeye's theme song, "I'm Popeye the Sailor Man," the song parodied in these verses, written by Sammy Lerner in 1934. For an instance of Donald Duck associated with garbage, see Chapter Six. We also collected a counting rhyme on the same theme: "I was born in a garbage can, just to see how old I am (counts)." Informant, Kristina, North Little Rock, Arkansas, age ten in 1993. Version Two can also be found in Joanna Coles's *Miss Mary Mack*.

5. *Astro Boy*, first shown in syndication in 1963, featured the title character, a robot. Produced by the same people who did *Speed Racer*, it was the first imported Japanimation to be a success in the United States.

6. Davy Crockett was an ongoing segment of the *Disneyland* television show that ran between 1954 and 1955. The show was a tremendous success, spawning a craze for coonskin caps and frontier memorabilia. David Crockett was a frontiersman from Tennessee with a gift for self-promotion who served under Andrew Jackson in the Indian wars. He served in the House of Representatives on and off in the early 19th century, and he died fighting at the Alamo. The television show highlighted his exploits as an Indian fighter, Congressman, and Alamo defender, starred Fess Parker, and sported a lengthy theme song which became a huge pop hit in 1955. "The Ballad of Davy Crockett" was written by Tom Blackburn and George Bruns in 1955. Four different versions competed on the pop charts, and one recorded by Bill Hayes held the number one spot for five weeks. Children wasted no time in adding on stanzas the original songwriters had never intended.

Version One is one in a subcategory of Davy Crockett parodies that feature a hero not as a wholesome frontiersman but as a violent urban criminal who got his start in particularly grim surroundings. This verse is similar in theme to celebrations of bad behavior in found in Chapter Five, but serves to humble a hero rather than one's classmate. It is effective because of the sharp contrast between the actions of the upright do-gooder Davy Crockett presented on the show and the nasty behavior and milieu presented in the rhymes. This urbanization and villainizing of Davy Crockett is found both in American and Great Britain; similar versions were collected at several English and Scottish sites in the 1950s by folklorists Iona and Peter Opie. See their *The Lore and Language of Schoolchildren* which, though dated, is an intriguing look at British children's subversive lore. The reference to DDT in Version One reflects the paranoia about that chemical bug killer prevalent at the time. The particular gun referred to, however, is a very old one, a British service rifle first used in 1895 and through World War II.

Version Two is more a parody of a commercial for a popular brand of cereal than a cut-down of Davy Crockett. Placing Crockett in a science-fictional milieu, however, does serve to render him silly.

Version Three is also silly, a "gotcha" rhyme setting up the listener for the punchline revelation. Mogen David is a brand of Kosher wine. Boys normally become bar-mitzvahed—the ritual act of taking on adult responsibilities—when they pass through puberty, usually taken to be age twelve or thirteen.

7. The 1950s and 1960s were the heyday of the television Western series (at one point there were more than thirty prime-time westerns in one season), of which *Branded* starring Chuck Connors, about a soldier unjustly dishonorably discharged for cowardice, was one (ran 1965-1966). The show is long gone, but the parody, as is often the case, remains. Versions Two and Three attack the cowboy's virility, asking what a "real man" would do in silly or offensive situations. Version Three serves the additional purpose of insulting someone you don't like. (For more insult rhymes, see Chapter Four.)

Versions Four and Five address the premise of the actual show and fall into a different rhythm; possibly they were sung to the chorus of the theme song. They point up the failure of the American justice system.

8. The *Howdy Doody Show* (ran from 1947-1960) starred "Buffalo" Bob Smith and appropriated the tune of "Ta Ra Ra Boom Der Ay" for its theme song. For other variations on this tune, see Chapter One. As a show aimed at kids, with a mix of live action characters (Buffalo Bob), puppets, and some modest interaction with actual kids in the audience the ("Peanut Gallery"), it was in many ways a precursor to *Barney*. The insertion of Frankenstein in the last line is probably a convenient rhyme that also serves as a horrific antidote to the wholesome goodness of the red-haired puppet-boy. (*Frankenstein* was first filmed in 1931 and the characters developed in the movie were used again and again from then until 1994, when a movie version was made by Kenneth Branaugh that attempted to adhere closer to Mary Shelley's original novel. The only daytime television show that actually featured Frankenstein was a short-running cartoon, *Frankenstein, Jr. & The Impossibles*, which ran in the same time slot as reruns of *Howdy Doody*, but six years later, in 1966.)

9. *The Addams Family* (ran 1964-1966): So weird they were cool—but still one wanted to distance oneself from them, hence they were all called "retarded." "Retarded" is probably being used colloquially to mean "dorky" rather than "mentally handicapped."

The characters and settings in the television were based on Charles Addams' cartoons for *The New Yorker*. Two Addams Family movies have been made in the 1990s starring Raul Julia and Angelica Huston, part of a wave of film-length treatments of 1960s and '70s children's television shows.

10. *The Brady Bunch* (ran 1969-1974) was a "modern" *Ozzie and Harriet* for the seventies, about the trials and tribulations in melding two families

together, something the first generation of the children of widespread divorce had to deal with. (On the show, however, each first spouse had died.) The Addams family was weird but cool; the Brady bunch was so normal it was weird. There's an element of self-hatred in making fun of this show, and a dig at the sensitive Mr. Brady, a "lady" and "jello" according to this version. Note that in the second verse the parody retains the original song's nice paradox of living together yet being alone. (The song was written by Sherwood Schwartz and Frank DeVol and is copyright by Addax Music Company, 1969.)

11. Unlike the other earlier television shows parodied above, *Sesame Street* (first aired in New York, 1969; first shown on national television, 1970) is not a network production. It is aired on public television and created by the Children's Television Workshop. It's aimed strictly at children, with no particular attempt to engage adults, and features a fast-paced mix of live action segments, cartoons, the late Jim Henson's muppets, and memorable songs (from the beginning using pop tunes like the Beatles' "Octopus's Garden"): a mix that anticipates MTV's format.

   This verse, lacking sexual innuendo, violence, or gross-outs, has the feel of an adult parody rather than a true children's rhyme. Another informant tells us that *Mad Magazine* ran a parody with similar lyrics with a reference to "Reality Street" in the last line. *Mad* and Tom Lehrer seem to be the two sources most responsible for ditties people think are folklore, but are in fact composed works.

12. *Sesame Street's* didactic approach is being parodied here, but note that these verses could also be used to insult the person being sung to.

13. *Sesame Street* went into territory where its predecessors such as *Mr. Rogers' Neighborhood* and *Captain Kangaroo* wouldn't dare to go. This is the response to the invasion of TV into the bathroom.

14. These verses suggest that the teller has mastered such adult concepts as violence, obscenities, childbirth, bestiality, and wife beating.

15. As Asimov postulates in his *Treasury of Humor*, the essence of humor is the twist of the unexpected: "The alteration in point of view produces an incongruity which elicits a laugh and a feeling of pleasure. The sharper the incongruity and the more suddenly it can be introduced, the more certain the laugh and louder and longer it will be."

   These verses are similar in format to the surprise ending ditties in Chapter Two. We also collected an adult version of a nursery rhyme:

> Hickory, Dickory Dock,
> A louse ran up the clock
> To half of a million
> Then dropped out of the bidding.
> Hickory, Dickory f___!

♦ *Dan, who heard it at an auction house in Los Angeles in 1992.*

16. These parodies are based on a poem by Sarah Joseph Hale, editor of *Godey's Lady's Book*, written in 1830.

17. This verse manages to combine a parody of a cute kiddie rhyme and taboo sex (bestiality) with a tongue twister in the fifth line!

18. Joanna Coles' *Miss Mary Mack* contains a less offensive comeback to an insult that also uses "Twinkle Twinkle Little Star."

19. It took until 1931 for Congress to make "The Star-Spangled Banner" the official anthem, which may also have something to do with the large number of other songs with special patriotic significance to Americans.

    That Americans are so comfortable making fun of their own institutions illustrates one of the conflicting themes in American character. From the start of our country there have been two streams of political thought, perhaps most easily identified by two heroic icons—call them the Federalist and the Cowboy. The first is comfortable with central power, and bestows upon government institutions an almost religious trust; the second rebels against restrictions and relentlessly questions any authority but his own. Both these ideals are praised in school, and, as can be seen above in the choice of heroes parodied, in the popular imagination. Perhaps it is because of these intertwined, sometimes conflicting ideals that there are so many American subversive rhymes on so many different themes.

20. Underwear rears its ugly head again. See Chapter Four for insult rhymes involving underwear, especially the variations using "The Old Grey Mare" tune. In these cases, the point of the verse does not seem to be to attack anyone for having only one pair of underwear since it is the singer whose underwear is mentioned. "God Bless America" was written by Irving Berlin in 1939.

21. "Over There" was written by George M. Cohan in 1917. The first version is more clearly a parody than the second, which seems to be making fun of the lesson that all people are the same under the skin, or at least, under their street clothes.

22. These are two of the few ditties using this tune that have nothing to do with teachers or school. For those that do see Chapter Five. Version One is actually a parody of a parody: There is a paratrooper's song about the fatal misadventures of a fellow whose 'chute failed to open, leaving him in a sorry condition much like the skier in this song. How the song made it from the military to the Girl Scouts is a matter for speculation. Possibly a child simply changed the protagonist from the less-familiar parachutist to the more common skier.

23. "This Land is Your Land" was written in 1956 by Woody Guthrie. The sentiments of the parody are exactly the opposite of the songwriter's words. Children may yield to parental wishes about sharing, but they are

not soft-hearted about it, especially as children realize that adults are possessive too. Children are, at a very early age, highly possessive of their playthings, their families, and by extension, their homes. Adults fight over national or ethnic matters, and they also fight over land. It is hardly surprising that children would pick up on the American territorial passion and make rhymes about both that and the sometimes violent fate of trespassers.

In Version Three note the use of "ain't" rather than the grammatically correct "it is" constructions of the other versions. Version Three, the most recent version collected, is also both more complete and more graphically violent than the others. That a ten year old knows the song well enough to parody it is possibly due to the resurgence of politically and ecologically correct messages in the media and schoolroom. For similarly violent reactions to such messages, see Chapter Nine on the deaths of Barney.

The parodying process sometimes continues into adulthood. Informant Dan, from West Virginia, notes that as a folksinger in the late 1960s, he would often sing: "This land is my land/ And don't forget it." He would then stop short, "leaving all the listeners with their hands in mid-clap."

Another informant shared with us the following variant, which he learned while in the Army in the sixties.

> This land is their land,
> This land ain't my land,
> From the Mekong delta
> To the Pleiku highland;
> When they get shot at,
> The ARVN flee,
> This land was made for the VC.

◆ *Jim from Bedford, New York, who learned it in the Army in the 1960s.*

24. The ubiquitous gopher makes his appearance yet again! Note that Popeye also is at home in a garbage can.

25. For more versions of "My Bonnie" see Chapters One and Two. This seems to be the case of a tune so versatile and well known that it is put to all sorts of uses.

26. In the early 1950s, Tom Lehrer also wrote a song, "The Irish Ballad," making fun of the grim themes to be found in many Irish folk songs.

27. For more about the history of "The Old Grey Mare" and the transfer of the melody into the tune of "Greasy Grimy Gopher Guts," see Chapter Five. The fact that the protagonist is a horse doesn't seem to matter in

this rhyme, which features the sniggering delights of someone losing her underwear. Or possibly "the old grey mare" is a sneer at an old woman, like the image of "granny losing her underwear" found in several verses in Chapter Four.

28. This parody refers, of course, to the smoking of marijuana, in which inhalation of the smoke is necessary for a "high." The use of marijuana, although some parents try to deny it, is found across the country even among preteens. For a more innocuous parody of "Row, Row, Row Your Boat," see Chapter Three. For less innocuous anti-teacher parodies, see Chapter Five.

29. For another variant on "Havah Nagila" see Chapter Six.

30. This is a parody of a Hebrew folksong, the lyrics of which consist entirely of: (loosely transliterated) "David Meloch Yisroel, chai chai ve'khyahm," which roughly translated means "David King of Israel, long may he reign." Sung in yeshivas in New York as a folk tune, it is also sung in Israel as a song of protest, having associations with the Jewish messianic idea of the coming of a new Jewish reign. The tune and song are probably dated to the early nineteenth century and the early Zionist period.

Our source for the above information also provided us with a local parody of another repetitive Hebrew song, this one sung at Passover. Transliterated, the parody is rendered, "Avadim hayeenu, Beh N.Y.C.Q." which translates to "Slaves we were in N.Y.C.Q." the initials representing their school, the Yeshiva Central Queens. We learned this from Moshe, 13-17 years old in 1965-69.

31. The show *Happy Days* (ran 1974-1984) used the hit version of "Rock Around the Clock" sung by Bill Haley and His Comets (1954). Ron Howard starred as Richie Cunningham, a completely normal joe going to high school in Milwaukee in the 1950s. The "normal" family was back—but only as a historical artifact.

32. "California Girls," written in 1965, was one in a long line of "dreaming of California" songs by Brian Wilson and recorded by his group celebrating the California lifestyle, the Beach Boys.

33. "Yesterday" was written by John Lennon and Paul McCartney, 1965. The Beatles were, of course, the most popular group of the 1960s, displacing Elvis in the hearts of American women and heralding the age of rock music as we know it. Not all teenage boys, however, were as taken by the Fab Four as their female counterparts. Hence, probably, this attack. For variants on "Yesterday" involving leprosy and diarrhea see Chapter Three.

34. "Hey Jude" was written by Paul McCartney in 1968. This parody is possibly referring to the infamous naked wedding bed photos of John and Yoko from 1969, John Lennon being the "Jude" in the song.

35. "Puff (the Magic Dragon)," a song about a little boy and a friendly drag-on, was written in 1963 by Peter Yarrow and Leonard Lipton and record-ed by Yarrow's group Peter, Paul, and Mary. The song was accused of promoting drug usage by some who thought the title character referred to marijuana smoking. Despite the mention of many items associated with Jewish life, this parody verse doesn't seem offensive enough to be intend-ed as a racial slur. For a similar listing of "other Jewish stuff," see above, Version Three of the parody of "The Ballad of Davy Crockett."

36. In this parody we see a contrast between the free and easy jungle life of Tarzan and the complicated, machine-ridden life of the modern age with such things as rubber bands, aeroplanes, and freeway lanes in it. The image of Tarzan swinging through the jungle is brought up short by the introduction of practical and dangerous considerations. This theme of showing the darker side of romantic, bucolic images is also found in many of the verses collected in this volume (see also Note 6 of this chap-ter on "Davy Crockett"). And the rhyme of "Cheetah" with "amoeba" is certainly an inventive one. Joanna Coles collected a two-line surprise end-ing verse in *Miss Mary Mack*, op. cit., of the sort found above in which Tarzan simply falls down

37. Tarzan started life as the hero of pulp adventures by Edgar Rice Burroughs, published initially in the 1930s. He has since had an active career in the movies starting with a silent feature in 1917, moving on to a series of silent shorts from 1928, going on to black and white movies with Johnny Weismuller and Buster Crabbe as the ape-man, and appearing in color in 1981 with a film featuring Bo Derek as Jane. He has been fea-tured in comic books continuously since the 1960s, as well. Tarzan, like Sherlock Holmes, Frankenstein's monster, and Dracula, has gone from being a mere literary creation to an icon recognized throughout Western culture. But this noble savage gets no relief from those most savage of all: kids.

38. In this assault on authority, Batman is cut down to size by a superior superhero icon, Superman. (Both Batman and Superman are published in comic books by DC Comics, and both Batman and Superman had their own television shows, though the treatment of the Superman show of the 1950s was very straight, in sharp contrast to Batman's.) For a similar treatment of Barney, see also the final verse of Chapter Nine. The garbage can most often associated with Popeye makes an appearance in this verse, as does Tarzan's rubber band.

39. As an example of its power over Generation X, a Nissan commercial in the spring of 1995 makes use of the theme from *Batman*.

40. Batman doesn't have a superpower *per se*; he is simply portrayed as being omni-competent, with a gadget—usually self-invented—for every occa-sion. Thus children cut him down to size not only by accusing him of

smelling, a traditional childish taunt (see Chapter Four and Chapter Three), but also by showing his best gadget, the Batmobile, breaking down and enabling the bad guy's escape. "Laid an egg" is a euphemism for farting. Version Three, the Jamaican variant, is interesting for the rural reference in the last line not found in the mainland versions. For many more parodies of Christmas tunes, see Chapter Six.

41. *King Kong* was first filmed in 1933 starring Fay Wray. A color remake was done in 1976 starring Jessica Lange. The character of Kong was also used in the 1950s and 1960s in low-grade Japanese monster films. Unlike the other cultural icons mentioned above, he never had the benefit of a literary incarnation (although the original movie was "novelized"). Nevertheless the image of the giant ape swinging from the spire of the Empire State Building, gently holding Fay Wray, was so powerful King Kong overcame that deficiency to become firmly embedded in the popular imagination.

   In this verse however, the powerful ape is reduced to sitting forlorn in the jungle, defeated by a mere banana.

CHAPTER NINE

1. Reportedly over one hundred million dollars in 1993.

2. The theme songs of television shows frequently serve as introductions to the concept behind the story, as in the cases of *Branded* and *The Brady Bunch*. Yet it is not Barney's introductory song that incites parody, even though the tune of "Yankee Doodle" frequently serves as the vehicle for subversive rhymes (see Chapters Four and Eight).

3. For instance, college students, such as those at the University of Nebraska, had a "Barney Bashing Day." A North Carolina radio preacher put out a pamphlet titled Barney the Purple Messiah, charging that Barney was out to introduce America's youth to the occult. Both of these instances of negative reaction to Barney were highly publicized by the news media.

4. Notice for instance the overuse of the word "love." The children at the center are not, in fact, a family, and there's no reason to expect them to act like one. Certainly friends should behave well toward one another, but the stanza about friends, less significant than the first stanza it follows, merely presents a tautology rather than a real guide to behavior.

5. Barney is dead but his message of cooperation lives on: many of these parodies involve getting together to kill Barney. This is a conspiracy, no lone gunmen here. It's also a nice satiric twist that Barney's message of cooperation should result in his downfall. Versions One, Three, Four,

Five, and Ten all end with a burst of enthusiasm for Barney's death. This is a direct parody of the enforced joy that Barney seeks from the children on the show for every single activity proposed. It is also slightly eerie to see the smiles on the children's faces during the entire time they are on screen.

There is no such thing as "9-9 mm gun," the vehicle of death in Version Two. Probably he meant a 9mm pistol. Nor is there such a gun as an 8-16 (Version Three). Possibly the child is confusing it with an M16 submachine gun. There was, at the turn of the century, a 4-16 gun, a bolt action elephant rifle that would surely take down Barney, but it is doubtful this is the origin.

Versions Five and Six put Barney in a tree. This is probably a "hanging tree," but the words may also be an obscure reference to "tree huggers," a mildly derogatory term for environmentalists, another breed of politically correct animal.

Version Eleven is the only variant of this song that involves the safe authority figure, Barney, turning on the children and committing violence first. In the next section he is accused of even more horrible things. The sentiment expressed in Version Twelve, the desire to kick Barney out of TV, is quite adult and it is interesting that it is one of our youngest informants who provides us with this variant.

6. In fact, a trend toward increased graphic violence in children's rhymes is something this collection of verse seems to have illustrated. Renatus Hartogs in *Anatomy of the Four Letter Word* and the more recent historical study by Geoffrey Hughes, *Swearing: A Social History of Oaths and Profanity in English*, have both documented the change in English swearing over the centuries from profanity to obscenity. As what is defined as obscene ever more blends into violence and death in popular culture (note the popularity of Madonna's S&M videos, S&M images in advertising, movies such as *Basic Instinct*, and so on), perhaps we are seeing in these children's rhymes where lines of taboo will be drawn in the future.

7. Adult versions usually insert the word "dysfunctional" before family.

8. As with Version Twelve above, Barney turns violent. His modus operandi is not terribly horrific, however. In the original song, Barney comes from "our Imagination," not outer space. For a similar mocking science-fictional treatment of Davy Crockett, see Chapter Eight. An informant tells us another anti-Barney hand-clapping verse to the tune of "Yankee Doodle" was published in *Cracked Magazine*.

9. Not only AIDS awareness is in evidence here, but also a sophisticated knowledge of such popular talk show discussion topics as child abuse and rape. While examples of coercive sex can certainly be found in

rhymes from earlier decades, it is up to our age to make so explicit and familiar to children the horrors of child abuse and rape that they are parodied in commonly known ditties.

H.I.V. is the virus commonly believed to be the precursor to AIDS. Baby Bop is another anthropomorphized dinosaur character, even more neotenous than Barney, who visits Barney almost every show. Their clan relationship is not clear, although their costumes suggest them to be from different species. There are no characters identified as gay or lesbian in the TV show.

We found this sample, another example of the ubiquity of these rhymes, in the November 11, 1993 issue of Rolling Stone, in a review by Chuck Eddy of the album Barney's Favorites, Vol. 1. He attributes the rhyme to third graders.

"I hate you,
You hate me,
You almost gave me HIV,
With a great big punch and a kick from me to you,
Won't you say you hate me, too?"

While the mention of HIV suggests that this might be one of the huge number of parodies made up by adults, the violence in the fourth line is in fact more typical of the parodies collected from children. Supporting that conclusion is a fragment of a verse reported to us by another informant, who tells us of overhearing a boy of about eight declaiming the following under the rotunda of the Capitol building: "I love you,/ You love me,/ Barney gave me HIV ..." His parents quieted him before he could finish the rest. Eddy notes that the Barney album made it onto the Billboard list of Top 20 albums. Anti-dino T-shirts are available from the "Funny Side Up" mail order catalog with this verse: "I hate you, you hate me,/ let's hang that dino from a tree," and a cartoon of the bottom half of a purple dinosaur, a tree, and a rope ($15.98).

There was, for a time, a "Kill Barney" topic on the GEnie network, with similar topics on all the major public bulletin boards. Several topics on the Internet have also been devoted to Barney, the prime example being "Alt.Barney.Die.Die.Die." Now we know how the Information Superhighway is really being used!

10. Barney's songs are usually accompanied by some sort of "Follow the Leader" style dance, and the dance of the sisters fit in quite well with the format of the TV show. For more Christmas parodies, see Chapter Six.

11. This is a glorious example of accretion in folklore. The verse starts with a hand clapping rhyme making reference to a simple written game (tic tac

toe), then kills off one of the biggest new popular culture figures by means of another older one, adds a line from another subversive rhyme (see Chapter Two for more about doctors and what they say), reverts to *very* old forms of the English language with the "be he" construction, makes a reference to the folktale of "Jack and the Bean Stalk" tale type, and ends merrily with a counting series.

BIBLIOGRAPHY

Asimov, Isaac. *Isaac Asimov's Treasury of Humor: A Lifetime Collection of Favorite Jokes, Anecdotes, and Limericks with Copious Notes on How to Tell Them and Why.* (Boston: Houghton Mifflin, 1971).

Bronner, Simon J. *American Children's Folklore.* (Little Rock: August House, 1988).

Brunvand, Jan Harold. *The Choking Doberman and Other "New" Urban Legends.* (New York: Norton, 1984).

Bryson, Bill. *Made in America.* (London: Secker & Warburg, 1994).

Butler, Francelia. *Skipping Around the World.* (New York: Ballantine Books, 1989).

Cole, Joanna. *Anna Banana: One Hundred and One Jump-Rope Rhymes.* (New York: Beech Tree Books, 1989).

Cole, Joanna and Stephanie Calmenson. *Miss Mary Mack and Other Children's Street Rhymes.* (New York: Beech Tree Books, 1991).

Joseph P. Goodwin. *More Man Than You'll Ever Be: Gay Folklore and Acculturation in Middle America.* (Bloomington: Indiana University Press, 1989).

Hartogs, Renatus, M.D., Ph.D., with Hans Fantel. *Four-Letter Word Games: The Psychology of Obscenity.* (New York: M.Evans and Company, 1967).

Hastings, Scott E., Jr. *Miss Mary Mac All Dressed in Black: Children's Lore from New England.* (Little Rock: August House, 1990).

Hughes, Geoffrey. *Swearing: A Social History of Oaths and Profanity in English.* (Oxford: Basil Blackwell, Ltd, 1991).

Kennedy, Peter, ed. *Folksongs of Britain and Ireland.* (Oak Publications, 1975).

Knapp, Mary and Herbert. *One Potato, Two Potato: The Folklore of American Children.* (New York: W.W. Norton and Company, 1976).

Legman, G. *No Laughing Matter: Rationale of the Dirty Joke, An Analysis of Sexual Humor, Second Series.* (New York: Bell Publishing Company, 1965).

Mechling, Jay. *"Children's Folklore"* in *Folk Groups and Folklore Genres: An Introduction,* edited by Elliott Oring (Logan, Utah: Utah State University Press, 1986).

Opie, Iona and Peter. *I Saw Esau: The Schoolchild's Pocket Book.* (Cambridge, Mass.: Candlewick Press, 1992). (Revision of *I Saw Esau: Traditional Rhymes of Youth from 1947*).

Opie, Iona and Peter. *The Lore and Language of Schoolchildren.* (London: Oxford University Press, 1959).

Percelay, James, Stephan Dweck and Monteria Ivey. *Snaps.* (Quill Books, New York, 1993).

Percelay, James, Stephan Dweck and Monteria Ivey. Introduction by Geneva Smitherman. *Double Snaps.* (New York: Quill Books, 1994).

Riordan, James. *The Sun Maiden and the Crescent Moon: Siberian Folk Tales.* (Edinburgh: Canongate Limited Publishing, 1989).

Sherman, Josepha. *A Sampler of Jewish-American Folklore.* (Little Rock: August House, 1992).

Silverman, Jerry. *The Dirty Song Book.* (New York, S/X Press, 1982).

Tuleja, Tad. *The New York Public Library Book of Popular Americana.* (New York: Macmillan, 1994).

Other Books from August House Publishers

Once upon a Galaxy

The ancient stories that inspired Star Wars, Superman, and other popular fantasies

Josepha Sherman

Hardback $19.95 / ISBN 0-87483-386-8

Paperback $11.95 / ISBN 0-87483-387-6

Rachel the Clever

And Other Jewish Folktales

Josepha Sherman

Hardback $18.95 / ISBN 0-87483-306-X

Paperback $10.95 / ISBN 0-87483-307-8

The Storytellers Start-Up Book

Finding, Learning, Performing, and Using Folktales

Margaret Read MacDonald

Hardback $23.95 / ISBN 0-87483-304-3
Paperback $13.95 / ISBN 0-87483-305-1

Queen of the Cold-Blooded Tales

Roberta Simpson Brown

Paperback $9.95 / ISBN 0-87483-408-2

Buried Treasures of the Pacific Northwest

W.C. Jameson

Paperback $11.95 / ISBN 0-87483-438-4

Race with Buffalo

and Other Native American Stories for Young Readers

Collected by Richard and Judy Dockrey Young

Hardback $19.95 / ISBN 0-87483-343-4
Paperback $9.95 / ISBN 0-87483-342-6

AUGUST HOUSE PUBLISHERS, INC.
P.O. BOX 3223
LITTLE ROCK, AR 72203
1-800-284-8784